Battleground Europe

ATLANTIC WALL
Pas de Calais

A German 37mm PaK 36 anti-tank gun positioned in a concrete firing pit. These small-calibre weapons were hopelessly obsolete against anything but light armour by 1944.

Battleground series:

Stamford Bridge & Hastings *by* Peter Marren
Wars of the Roses - Wakefield / Towton *by* Philip A. Haigh
Wars of the Roses - **Barnet** *by* David Clark
Wars of the Roses - **Tewkesbury** *by* Steven Goodchild
Wars of the Roses - **The Battles of St Albans** *by*
Peter Burley, Michael Elliott & Harvey Wilson
English Civil War - **Naseby** *by* Martin Marix Evans, Peter Burton
and Michael Westaway
English Civil War - **Marston Moor** *by* David Clark
War of the Spanish Succession - **Blenheim 1704** *by* James Falkner
War of the Spanish Succession - **Ramillies 1706** *by* James Falkner
Napoleonic - **Hougoumont** *by* Julian Paget and Derek Saunders
Napoleonic - **Waterloo** *by* Andrew Uffindell and Michael Corum
Zulu War - **Isandlwana** *by* Ian Knight and Ian Castle
Zulu War - **Rorkes Drift** *by* Ian Knight and Ian Castle
Boer War - **The Relief of Ladysmith** *by* Lewis Childs
Boer War - **The Siege of Ladysmith** *by* Lewis Childs
Boer War - **Kimberley** *by* Lewis Childs

Mons *by* Jack Horsfall and Nigel Cave
Néry *by* Patrick Tackle
Le Cateau *by* Nigel Cave and Jack Shelden
Walking the Salient *by* Paul Reed
Ypres - **Sanctuary Wood and Hooge** *by* Nigel Cave
Ypres - **Hill 60** *by* Nigel Cave
Ypres - **Messines Ridge** *by* Peter Oldham
Ypres - **Polygon Wood** *by* Nigel Cave
Ypres - **Passchendaele** *by* Nigel Cave
Ypres - **Airfields and Airmen** *by* Mike O'Connor
Ypres - **St Julien** *by* Graham Keech
Ypres - **Boesinghe** *by* Stephen McGreal
Walking the Somme *by* Paul Reed
Somme - **Gommecourt** *by* Nigel Cave
Somme - **Serre** *by* Jack Horsfall & Nigel Cave
Somme - **Beaumont Hamel** *by* Nigel Cave
Somme - **Thiepval** *by* Michael Stedman
Somme - **La Boisselle** *by* Michael Stedman
Somme - **Fricourt** *by* Michael Stedman
Somme - **Carnoy-Montauban** *by* Graham Maddocks
Somme - **Pozières** *by* Graham Keech
Somme - **Courcelette** *by* Paul Reed
Somme - **Boom Ravine** *by* Trevor Pidgeon
Somme - **Mametz Wood** *by* Michael Renshaw
Somme - **Delville Wood** *by* Nigel Cave
Somme - **Advance to Victory (North) 1918** *by* Michael Stedman
Somme - **Flers** *by* Trevor Pidgeon
Somme - **Bazentin Ridge** *by* Edward Hancock
Somme - **Combles** *by* Paul Reed
Somme - **Beaucourt** *by* Michael Renshaw
Somme - **Redan Ridge** *by* Michael Renshaw
Somme - **Hamel** *by* Peter Pedersen
Somme - **Villers-Bretonneux** *by* Peter Pedersen
Somme - **Airfields and Airmen** *by* Mike O'Connor
Airfields and Airmen of the Channel Coast *by* Mike O'Connor
In the Footsteps of the Red Baron *by* Mike O'Connor
Arras - **Airfields and Airmen** *by* Mike O'Connor
Arras - **The Battle for Vimy Ridge** *by* Jack Sheldon & Nigel Cave
Arras - **Vimy Ridge** *by* Nigel Cave
Arras - **Gavrelle** *by* Trevor Tasker and Kyle Tallett
Arras - **Oppy Wood** *by* David Bilton
Arras - **Bullecourt** *by* Graham Keech
Arras - **Monchy le Preux** *by* Colin Fox
Walking Arras *by* Paul Reed
Hindenburg Line *by* Peter Oldham
Hindenburg Line - **Epehy** *by* Bill Mitchinson
Hindenburg Line - **Riqueval** *by* Bill Mitchinson
Hindenburg Line - **Villers-Plouich** *by* Bill Mitchinson
Hindenburg Line - **Cambrai Right Hook** *by* Jack Horsfall & Nigel Cave
Hindenburg Line - **Cambrai Flesquières** *by* Jack Horsfall & Nigel Cave
Hindenburg Line - **Saint Quentin** *by* Helen McPhail and Philip Guest
Hindenburg Line - **Bourlon Wood** *by* Jack Horsfall & Nigel Cave
Cambrai - **Airfields and Airmen** *by* Mike O'Connor
Aubers Ridge *by* Edward Hancock

La Bassée - Neuve Chapelle *by* Geoffrey Bridger
Loos - **Hohenzollern Redoubt** *by* Andrew Rawson
Loos - **Hill 70** *by* Andrew Rawson
Fromelles *by* Peter Pedersen
The Battle of the Lys 1918 *by* Phil Tomaselli
Accrington Pals Trail *by* William Turner
Poets at War: Wilfred Owen *by* Helen McPhail and Philip Guest
Poets at War: Edmund Blunden *by* Helen McPhail and Philip Guest
Poets at War: Graves & Sassoon *by* Helen McPhail and Philip Guest
Gallipoli *by* Nigel Steel
Gallipoli - **Gully Ravine** *by* Stephen Chambers
Gallipoli - **Anzac Landing** *by* Stephen Chambers
Gallipoli - **Suvla August Offensive** *by* Stephen Chambers
Gallipoli - **Landings at Helles** *by* Huw & Jill Rodge
Walking the Italian Front *by* Francis Mackay
Italy - **Asiago** *by* Francis Mackay
Verdun: Fort Douamont *by* Christina Holstein
Verdun: Fort Vaux *by* Christina Holstein
Walking Verdun *by* Christina Holstein
Zeebrugge & Ostend Raids 1918 *by* Stephen McGreal

Germans at Beaumont Hamel *by* Jack Sheldon
Germans at Thiepval *by* Jack Sheldon

SECOND WORLD WAR

Dunkirk *by* Patrick Wilson
Calais *by* Jon Cooksey
Boulogne *by* Jon Cooksey
Saint-Nazaire *by* James Dorrian
Walking D-Day *by* Paul Reed
Atlantic Wall - **Pas de Calais** *by* Paul Williams
Atlantic Wall - **Normandy** *by* Paul Williams
Normandy - **Pegasus Bridge** *by* Carl Shilleto
Normandy - **Merville Battery** *by* Carl Shilleto
Normandy - **Utah Beach** *by* Carl Shilleto
Normandy - **Omaha Beach** *by* Tim Kilvert-Jones
Normandy - **Gold Beach** *by* Christopher Dunphie & Garry Johnson
Normandy - **Gold Beach Jig** *by* Tim Saunders
Normandy - **Juno Beach** *by* Tim Saunders
Normandy - **Sword Beach** *by* Tim Kilvert-Jones
Normandy - **Operation Bluecoat** *by* Ian Daglish
Normandy - **Operation Goodwood** *by* Ian Daglish
Normandy - **Epsom** *by* Tim Saunders
Normandy - **Hill 112** *by* Tim Saunders
Normandy - **Mont Pinçon** *by* Eric Hunt
Normandy - **Cherbourg** *by* Andrew Rawson
Normandy - **Commandos & Rangers on D-Day** *by* Tim Saunder
Das Reich – **Drive to Normandy** *by* Philip Vickers
Oradour *by* Philip Beck
Market Garden - **Nijmegen** *by* Tim Saunders
Market Garden - **Hell's Highway** *by* Tim Saunders
Market Garden - **Arnhem, Oosterbeek** *by* Frank Steer
Market Garden - **Arnhem, The Bridge** *by* Frank Steer
Market Garden - **The Island** *by* Tim Saunders
Rhine Crossing – **US 9th Army & 17th US Airborne** *by* Andrew R
British Rhine Crossing – **Operation Varsity** *by* Tim Saunders
British Rhine Crossing – **Operation Plunder** *by* Tim Saunders
Battle of the Bulge – **St Vith** *by* Michael Tolhurst
Battle of the Bulge – **Bastogne** *by* Michael Tolhurst
Channel Islands *by* George Forty
Walcheren *by* Andrew Rawson
Remagen Bridge *by* Andrew Rawson
Cassino *by* Ian Blackwell
Anzio *by* Ian Blackwell
Dieppe *by* Tim Saunders
Fort Eben Emael *by* Tim Saunders
Crete – **The Airborne Invasion** *by* Tim Saunders
Malta *by* Paul Williams
Bruneval Raid *by* Paul Oldfield
Cockleshell Raid *by* Paul Oldfield

Battleground Europe

ATLANTIC WALL
Pas de Calais

PAUL WILLIAMS

Pen & Sword
MILITARY

First published in Great Britain in 2013 by
Pen & Sword Military
an imprint of
Pen & Sword Books Ltd
47 Church Street
Barnsley
South Yorkshire
S70 2AS
Copyright © Paul Williams 2013
ISBN 9781848848177

Typeset in 10 pt Palatino by
Factionpress
Printed and bound by CPI Group (UK) Ltd, Croydon, CR0 4YY

Pen & Sword Books Ltd incorporates the Imprints of Pen & Sword
Aviation, Pen & Sword Maritime, Pen & Sword Military, Wharncliffe
Local History, Pen and Sword Select, Pen and Sword Military
Classics, Leo Cooper, Remember When, Seaforth Publishing and
Frontline Publishing.
For a complete list of Pen & Sword titles please contact
PEN & SWORD BOOKS LIMITED
47 Church Street, Barnsley, South Yorkshire, S70 2AS, England
E-mail: enquiries@pen-and-sword.co.uk
Website: www.pen-and-sword.co.uk

CONTENTS

	Introduction	6
	Glossary	8
Chapter One	Enemy at the Door	9
Chapter Two	Attack To Defence	29
Chapter Three	The Organisation Todt	45
Chapter Four	Construction Of The Atlantic Wall Bunkers	61
Chapter Five	The Founding of Hobart's 'Funnies'	91
Chapter Six	From Le Havre to Dunkerque	107
Chapter Seven	Fortress Or Folly? Conclusions	149
Chapter Eight	Atlantic Wall Sites in The Pas De Calais	157
	Acknowledgements	165
	Atlantic Wall in Maps and Plans	167
	Index	174

Feldmarschall Rommel discusses some problems of defending a French port with fortress commander *Generalmajor* Hünten and *General* Fahrmbacher, artillery commander.

INTRODUCTION

IF THE NORMANDY LANDINGS were the beginning of the end for Nazi Germany in Western Europe, the breakout from the Falaise Gap, south of Caen, was the end of the beginning of the end. The *Heer* made a final, desperate attempt to contain the Allied invasion in the area between the towns of Trun, Argentan and Vimoutiers but ended up being effectively destroyed as a fighting force.

The battle of the Falaise Gap marked the end of the Battle of Normandy, which started 6 June 1944, and ended 22 August 1944. Although 100,000 Germans succeeded in escaping the Allies, they still left behind 150,000 prisoners and wounded and over 10,000 dead. British, American and Canadian troops swept eastwards and northwards, the stream of invading soldiers became a torrent.

By the late summer of 1944, Allied forces had begun clearing the fortified ports, Hitler's *Festunghäfe*, to the north. These ports and their layered, formidable defences formed an integral part of the Atlantic Wall. But like the rest of the barrier that the Germans had boasted was invincible, many of the guns pointed out to sea, anticipating any attack to come from the direction of the English Channel. From the landward side, they had little defence against overwhelming numbers but Hitler still demanded that every one of their garrison fight to the death in the vain hope that even a day's delay in opening up the channel ports would give his armies the chance to cut off the Allied supply lines and leave thousands of troops stranded and at the mercy of a counter-attack.

In the end, the capture of Antwerp rendered all German hopes of an Allied collapse redundant. The race to capture the Channel ports before the Germans had the chance to disable their facilities became less pressing. This is the story of how the Pas De Calais' offensive and defensive capabilities impacted the Second World War and why and how the region became the most heavily defended section in the Atlantic Wall.

TRAVEL ADVICE – PAS DE CALAIS

The ferry remains the most popular route for car drivers from England to France. Seafrance (http://www.seafrance.com) and P&O Ferries (HYPERLINK "http://www.poferries.com" http://www.poferries.com) both offer regular daily sailings

Rommel inspects the Pas de Calais defences.

between Dover and Calais and you are immediately within easy driving distance of most of the Pas de Calais Atlantic Wall sites. The sailing takes less than two hours nowadays.

However, a generally less expensive option is to use DFDS Seaways (HYPERLINK "http://www.dfdsseaways.co.uk" http://www.dfdsseaways.co.uk) who operate between Dover and Dunkerque. The sailing time is only slightly longer at around two hours and access from the port of Dunkerque onto the French motorway network is straightforward.

The other option, of course, is the Channel Tunnel (http://www.eurotunnel.com). This is the favourite of the non-sailors and normally guarantees you'll emerge at Sangatte well inside an hour. The route, however, continues to be relatively expensive unless you can travel well outside peak times.

By air, the options are very limited after BMI suspended its service to Lille from Leeds, though LyddAir http://www.lyddair.com http://www.lyddair.com) runs a weekend service by light aircraft to Cote de l'Opale airport at Le Touquet, south of Boulogne, from Lydd in Kent. The flight time is about 20 minutes.

From five-star hotels and guest houses to gites and campsites, there is a big choice of accommodation in the Pas de Calais and probably the best website from which to gather information and make bookings is http://www.visitfrance.co.uk, though http://www.ukcampsite.co.uk" http://www.ukcampsite.co.uk has some excellent recommendations for campers. I found the Chateau Du Gandspette (http://www.chateau-gandspette.com" http://www.chateau-gandspette.com) at Eperleques, between Calais and St Omer, to be an excellent base from which to explore the area.

GLOSSARY

ARK	Armoured Ramp Carrier
AVRE	Assault Vehicle Royal Engineers; an adapted tank designed to overcome defensive structures
Bangalore	Explosive charge
BARV	Beach Armoured Recovery Vehicle
Buffalo	Armoured landing craft or bulldozer
Carrot	Small explosive charge
Centaur	Armoured bulldozer
Chindits	British army units engaged in deep penetration of Japanese-held territory inBurma
Crab	Sherman tank with mine-clearing flails
Crocodile	Churchill tank with flame thrower
DUKW	Armoured amphibious carrier
Duplex Drive	Propelling system for 'swimming' tanks
Eisenbahn Batterie	Railway gun battery
Eiserne Hemmkurven	curved iron anti-tank obstacles
Fascine	Tank-mounted bridging device
Festung	Fortress
Festungpionier Korps	Fortress engineering corps
Flail	Tank-mounted mine-clearing chains
Flying Dustbin	High Explosive Squash Head projectile designed to pierce concrete
Gastarbeitnehmer	Guest employee – Slave labourer
Hafenkommandant	Port Commander
Kampfgruppen	Battle groups, *ad hoc* units hastily assembled
Kangaroo	Armoured personnel carrier
Kriegsmarine	German Navy
Luftwaffe	German Air Force
Landungsboot	Landing craft
Sprengfallen Artilleriegranaten	Booby-trapped artillery shells
Oberkommando des Heeres	German Army High Command
Offene Bettung (OB)	Open gun pit
Ostbataillone	Ex-Soviet POWs and other anti-Soviet volunteer
Panzerstellung	Concrete-ringed fixed tank turret position
Penny Packets	Small numbers
Petard	Technical name for the 'Flying Dustbin'
Pionier Langsdungboot	Landing craft as used by German engineers
Regelbau	Standard construction
Reichsarbeitsdienstmänner	Conscripted male civilian workers
Ringstände	Tobruk or ring-stand open gun-pt position
Sockellafetten	Gun pedestal mount
Sonderkonstruktion	Special construction
Turm	Tower or turret
Verstärkt feldmässig (Vf)	Reinforced open gun emplacement
Wehrmacht	German Armed Forces

Chapter One

ENEMY AT THE DOOR

THE ATLANTIC WALL was Hitler's infamous but ill-planned barrier between the Allies and Nazi-occupied mainland Europe. Intended to be impenetrable but fatally flawed, its relative inflexibility and very magnitude was to ultimately prove its Achilles heel.

The term 'Atlantic Wall' is an all-encompassing label but a fairly accurate one in that its function, albeit defined in stages, was to protect acquired German interests along more than 5,000 kilometres of coastline facing the north Atlantic. That included the coastlines of Norway, Denmark, Germany itself, The Netherlands, Belgium and France and incorporated the tip of the Barents Sea, the Norwegian Sea, the North Sea, the English Channel and the Bay of Biscay. In European terms the Atlantic Wall was rivalled only in size by the Maginot Line, France's vast network of fortifications built following the 1918 Armistice that was so cruelly exposed by Germany's blitzkrieg tactics at the beginning of the Second World War.

The Atlantic Wall in France was to cost the German taxpayer approximately 2.7 billion *Reichsmarks* (equivalent to 5.5 billion euros at the time of writing). Of course, that means little to the layman nowadays but to put the figure into some kind of context, the amount of steel used on construction sites in France was the same as was used in German tank production at the height of the war, or roughly one twentieth of the total steel production of Germany at that time. In addition, workers poured around 17.3 million cubic tons of concrete.

Northern France, of course, was the keystone to the Atlantic Wall. At first the planned launching point for an invasion of the British Isles (Operation *Seelöwe* [Sealion]), it was later to become pivotal in Hitler's plans to foil the Allied landings. Had the fortifications been integrated into Germany's overall military strategy, they would undoubtedly have been more effective. However, thankfully from an Allied point of view, this was not the case. Indeed 'The Wall' was to prove a constant area of conflict among the *Wehrmacht* hierarchy and with the Führer

Generalfeldmarschall Gerd von Runstedt checking the Atlantic Wall defences with a *Kriegsmarine* officer in 1944.

himself from the outbreak of war with Britain and its Allies to D-Day and beyond. Principally, as the manning of the fortifications severely hampered the German Army's ability to commit resources to where logic dictated they would be needed most in the event of an Allied landing in northern France.

Generalfeldmarschall Gerd von Runstedt, overall commander of the *Heer* in France from 1942 to 1944, was later to describe the Atlantic Wall as little more than propaganda for the masses, built to convince the German people that Hitler's *Festung Europa* was a reality and to act as a deterrent to the forces massing across the English Channel.

So how was the folly allowed to perpetuate for so long? Hitler's ego almost certainly had a big part to play in that, but to fully understand how 'The Wall' developed one has to wind the clock back, initially, to the beginning of the twentieth century.

Germany's coastal defence had, traditionally, been the responsibility of the *Kaiserliche Marine* (Imperial Navy) who, at the outbreak of the First World War, had designed an effective shield of warship and submarine patrols in the North Sea and Baltic Sea to protect the

Hitler was proud of his *Festung Europa* – a line of concrete defences from Norway to Spain.

ports of Bremerhaven, Hamburg, Kiel and Rostock. This was supplemented, closer to land, by torpedo boats and minefields with shore batteries on the coast as a final line of defence. The guns at this time were almost exclusively free-standing with little in the way of protection should they come under attack.

These tactics were fairly effective in protecting the Fatherland but proved to be less so when Germany occupied Belgium at the outset of the Great War of 1914-1918. The *Kaiserliche Marine* found itself in direct opposition to the Royal Navy, which had a massive presence in the North Sea and English Channel at that time. The Germans found themselves out-gunned and outnumbered when they confronted the Royal Navy head-on. They lacked the resources to target the British fleet from the

Belgian shoreline. So they turned to the army for help. One has to understand that present-day rivalry in many countries between the different branches of the armed forces verged on open hostility at the beginning of the twentieth century. Cooperation was almost unheard of between the army and navy. This was to prove a major hindrance in military terms, which the Nazi government was to exploit in the years ahead.

Construction of fortified gun emplacements, known as cauldron (*Kesselbettungen*) because of their pan-like shape on the ground, were built usually housing a 100 mm gun, though they offered little protection for gun crews.

Of course, the aftermath of the First World War put a temporary halt to the building of coastal fortifications, as did the worldwide recession during the 1920s. But the *Reichsmarine* stepped up its plans to fortify the German coastline again in the 1930s as Hitler began a massive re-arming, with the islands of Heligoland Bay becoming the first part of Nazi Germany to have modern fortifications built overlooking the sea.

Heligoland lies approximately seventy kilometres from the German coastline in the area of the North Sea known to devotees of the shipping forecast in Britain as German Bight. Once owned by both the Danish and the British, the islands were strategically important to the Germans in that they could

Heligoland with its early German defences.

give advance warning of anyone approaching the port of Hamburg from the sea though, of course, this importance became largely redundant with the development of the aeroplane. It can only be assumed, therefore, that the decision to fortify the islands was probably experimental (comparisons have been drawn to subsequent fortifications on the Channel Islands) as well as being a notice of intent.

The defences on Heligoland were eventually razed to the ground by the RAF in April 1945 (causing the population to abandon their homes) and the Royal Navy tried to wipe the islands off the map by detonating almost 7,000 tonnes of explosives there in 1947. They survived, however, and have now become a tourist destination. The present-day *Bundesmarine* ironically, operates an air-sea rescue centre from the harbour.

At the beginning of the Second World War, the *Kreigsmarine* still did not have a force tasked solely with coastal defence nor, indeed, a dedicated overall infrastructure. Instead, it was being left to regional command centres to orchestrate a policy to deal with the defence of their own particular stretch of coastline. The North Sea coast had batteries and anti-aircraft *FlaK* units at several points, but there were neither fortifications to link the outposts nor communication between the different units. However, France's capitulation and the Allies' retreat from Dunkirk in 1940 brought a new urgency to Germany's war effort and, with the *Heer* contemplating a landing on mainland Britain, Hitler issued fresh orders (Führer Directive No. 16) to create a string of fortified batteries along the coast of the Pas de Calais. These were intended to ensure Germany had command of the Straits of Dover in order to give maximum protection to Operation Sealion (*Seelöwe*), the amphibious invasion of England. It also meant that the *Heer* now had the authority to take control of Germany's offensive and defensive capabilities.

As the Battle of Britain raged overhead in the summer of 1940, the German Army began moving massive rail-mounted guns into the Pas de Calais region. These were typically long-range Krupp 203 mm and later the Skoda 210 mm guns.

The Krupp family had been making armaments for the German military for hundreds of years, developing the infamous Paris Gun in World War One which was widely regarded as the ultimate terror weapon of that era. During the 1930s, they diversified into the construction of tanks and

The infamous Paris Gun of the First World War. In action again as K5 in the Second World War.

submarines. Krupp was also responsible for the highly effective 88 mm anti-aircraft gun. However, long-range guns were their speciality and the 203 mm was to prove a potent weapon in the Pas de Calais.

The Paris Gun's sheer velocity had meant that its barrel life was limited to a mere fifty rounds and its shells had to have a numbered sequence of firing to allow for the rapid barrel wear. Krupp, therefore, came up with a design to machine splines on the shells of his new long-range guns to match grooves made in the barrel with a copper band, packed in by asbestos and graphite, sealing in the exhaust gasses. This allowed multiple firings and reduced maintenance costs. The designs worked and the first K (*Kanone*) 12 (E) went into manufacture and was delivered to the *Heer* in March 1939. Later designs included the K12 N (E) and K12 V (E) and, though generally superseded by the more efficient 280 mm K5 (E), which was developed alongside it, in 1940. The K12 remained in operation until 1944, seeing final service in the Italian campaign where it was used to shell the Allied landing forces at Anzio in January of that year.

Fragments of a shell fired from a K12 were unearthed in Chatham in Kent after the war, a distance of around 120 kilometres from Calais, which underlines the range of the gun.

Typical shell damage in Dover.

The K5 was to provide the backbone of the barrage on the south coast towns of England. However, preparing to fire these leviathans was an intricate task.

On arriving at its firing point, the handbrake on the front carriage of the gun had to be applied and the pressure hoses uncoupled. Hydraulics then raised the gun gondola and the rear truck was moved backwards and locked in place. The generator then had to be transferred to the rear truck from the ammunition supply car by means of rollers and pulleys before being secured. The track was then marked so that, after recoil, it could be repositioned at its original starting point. Mounted on a box-girder carriage and, in turn, on double bogies, a pneumatic recoil system allowed the entire ensemble to recoil a metre back along the track on firing. It took several bags of propellant to make the charge which fired the shell and all of it had to be rammed manually into the breech The barrel could then be aimed and the gun was fired by means of a lanyard, necessary as it was too dangerous to allow men on the carriage while the gun was being discharged. Incidentally the barrel itself had to have external support during transportation or it would have buckled under its own weight. Vögele turntables (*Drehscheibe*) were commonly utilised on the tracks between Calais and Boulogne to facilitate its firing, while a prefabricated T-shaped length of rail could also be carried on the gun train and

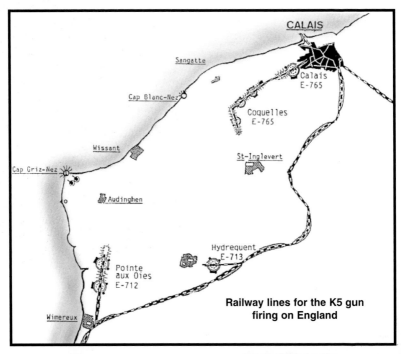

Railway lines for the K5 gun firing on England

deployed by a special crane to provide stability (the gun could not be fired on a straight piece of railway line because of the massive recoil). This also allowed the gun to be fired through 360 degrees. But, in connection with these giant rail guns, it was the building of the first *Dombunker* (cathedral bunkers) that was to be a sign of things to come.

The K5 could fire fifteen rounds an hour unimpeded but, of course, it was still highly vulnerable to attack from the RAF's fighters and fighter-bombers who, after all, were only a few minutes flying time from northern France. Tarpaulins and camouflage nets offering little defence against an eagle-eyed pilot. But in September 1940, construction began on several of these *Dombunker*, so called because of their initial resemblance to the arched roof of a Gothic cathedral. They were, in fact, no more than reinforced tunnels, usually about eighty metres in length and ten metres high.

The tunnels were cut into banks of earth and were dotted along the Pas de Calais coastline between Calais and Wimereux, the closest point on mainland Europe to the British coast. The site of one was at Fort Nieulay in the western suburbs of Calais.

Fort Nieulay was a seventeenth century stone fortress that was abandoned in the 1800s and had been converted into a farm and outbuildings by the time war broke out in 1939. But it was quickly to become a significant military site due to its location. The fort bisected the land between the main Calais to Boulogne road and the major coastal railway. It was the scene of a last stand by French and English troops ordered to defend the approach to the port of Calais in May 1940.

A small force of men (supported by Royal Navy ships off Cap Gris Nez) from the 3rd Battalion Royal Tank Regiment, who had already had most of their armour destroyed, and the

Fort Nieulay near Calais.

17

Queen Victoria's Rifles, who included several wounded among their ranks, held out for two days under mortar attack and shelling before being overrun by the *Schützenregiment 86* and the tanks of the *Panzerpionier Battalion 49*. But they'd bought vital time for troops in Calais itself, who managed to disable weaponry and evacuate before the Germans arrived.

In late summer of 1940, the *Heer* had nine *Eisenbahnbatterien* (railway battery regiments) manning sixteen separate railway guns. In addition, the *Kriegsmarine* had two 150 mm railway guns known as *Batterie Gneisnau*. But there was still some dispute over who should be targeting what. In the end, all the guns were put under the command of the new Army Artillery Command 104, though the *Kriegmarine* guns were still only to be allowed to fire on naval targets until the invasion of Britain was under way.

HELLFIRE CORNER

Perhaps it is not as well documented as it should be but the English south coast ports of Dover and Folkestone, in particular, were to be the target of significant bombardments between 1939 and 1944.

Folkestone had been subjected to 'tip and run', as the locals called them, air raids from the early days of hostilities. 'Tip and run' referred to the ploy of the *Luftwaffe* in flying at low altitude across the English Channel to avoid detection before dropping their payload on the unsuspecting people of the port before they could reach the air raid shelters. The planes could then turn tail and head back to their bases in northern France before Fighter Command could be mustered.

The Germans used raids like this to train young pilots and aircrew as they were at very little risk of being challenged. Unfortunately for them, it also meant that the bombers often missed their intended targets. Christ Church in Folkestone suffered a direct hit on Sunday 17 May 1942 just moments after a parade of military personnel had been stood down. The tower was the only part of the church to survive and now forms part of a Garden of Remembrance in the town.

From November 1942, Folkestone was subjected to frequent barrages from the K5s in the Pas de Calais. Worst hit was the lower part of the town around the harbour which became known as 'The Shelling'. A siren was sounded when the barrage began but, of course, there was no advance warning and no indication when the bombardment was over. An all-clear was usually sounded after an hour but the German gun crews became wise to this and would often fire again after 75 or 90 minutes, catching civilians in the open. But despite Folkestone's tribulations, it was still Dover that bore the brunt of the German aggression along the south coast.

Having recently survived the Dunkirk evacuation, followed by the Battle of Britain, the British did not have an immediate answer to this threat, but the high ground to either side of the Port of Dover was fortified on the personal order of the Prime Minister (who had visited to see the situation in person), and large calibre guns were dug in there. The only British cross-Channel guns already in place were 'Winnie' and – later in 1940 – 'Pooh' (named after the Prime Minister, Winston Churchill, and A. A. Milne's fictional bear). These were two 14-inch (35.6 cm) guns positioned behind St Margaret's on the Cliff. The guns were spares taken from Royal Navy surplus stores and intended to equip the battleship HMS *King George V*. As they needed mountings, surplus equipment again, this time from HMS

British heaavy guns at South Foreland Battery.

Furious, were utilised and the other gun used a mounting from a test range. Neither guns were housed in armoured turrets, and were therefore vulnerable to both air attack and shelling from the other side of the Channel. They was protected from aerial attack by anti-aircraft emplacements and had independent and well-camouflaged cordite magazines buried under several layers of earth. The guns were then linked to the magazine by an underground railway.

Operated from an unattached firing-control centre, Winnie and Pooh were typically manned by twenty-five man crews drawn from the Royal Marine Siege Regiment. It would be fair to say the guns at St Margaret's didn't have tremendous strategic value but their presence did wonders for morale on the south coast. It was Winnie that fired Britain's first land-based shell onto German-occupied continental Europe in August 1940. However, the British gun operation was slow and ineffective in comparison to the German railway and battery-based guns and they could only target fixed positions, meaning German shipping could traverse the Channel with relative impunity if it could avoid Royal Navy patrols.

This situation didn't please the British Prime Minster, however, who remained perplexed by the existing guns' lack of success in targeting shipping. Churchill, therefore, ordered three new heavy gun batteries to be built in Dover for that express purpose.

The new batteries were to be manned by the Royal Artillery and were sited at Fan Bay, South Foreland and Wanstone.

There were three 6-inch guns (15.2 cm) at Fan Bay, near St Margarets, with a range of 25,000 yards.

South Foreland battery (290 Coastal Battery) comprised two underground shelters (excavated in 1941 by 172 Tunnelling Company and No. 1 section, 171 Tunnelling Company Royal Engineers), two plotting or targeting areas and four ammunition stores for the four 9.2-inch (23.4 cm) guns. In addition, there were the normal above-ground facilities one associates with a medium-sized military position: they included kitchen, workshops, washrooms and stores. The guns themselves had a range of around seventeen miles.

But Wanstone, with its two 15-inch (38 cm) guns with a range of twenty-four miles, was the heaviest gun battery installed along the coastline of Kent during the Second World War,

Wanstone Battery (part of 540 Coast Defence Regiment) was also one of only two sites in the entire British Empire that mounted the huge 15-inch Coast Defence Guns. But, unlike their counterparts at Singapore, these guns never fell to an enemy attack. Like the 14-inch guns 'Winnie' and 'Pooh', these two guns also had nicknames – 'Jane' and 'Clem'.

It's believed that 'Jane' was named after the popular wartime cartoon strip character in the *Daily Mirror*, while 'Clem' was probably named for Clementine Churchill, Winston's wife. The primary purpose of the battery was to deny the free passage of Axis shipping in the English Channel, but the weapons were also able to operate in a counter-battery role if necessary by

Churchill looks out across the Channel from Dover Castle.

upping the amount of firing charge. They were to support the Canadian assault on the Atlantic Wall on D-Day. Unlike the majority of the German batteries that were eventually housed in casemates, the British guns were only protected by basic steel armour housings, relying heavily instead on camouflage, a reverse-slope siting and on air superiority preventing an attack by enemy aircraft.

The two guns were sited a distance away from each other to safeguard against residual damage should one or both suffer a direct hit and each was served by its own individual ammunition stores in huge surface magazines. Both remain today as humps on the landscape. Small tractor units transported the shells and charges from the magazines directly to the guns, enabling multi-firing. Unfortunately, however, the guns' design didn't tolerate continual use. Barrel erosion was an ongoing problem and the ramming mechanism frequently failed. So much so that a complete spare had to be kept on site.

Barrel wear, as mentioned above, was a serious problem that affected both the accuracy and range of the guns but by early 1944 Vickers had developed a technique to refurbish the barrels rather than continually replace them and, by D-Day, the guns could sustain 150 firings before any maintenance needed to be carried out.

The battery was provided with underground accommodation and medical services in a shelter dug in 1941 – two offset parallel tunnels each over sixty metres in length, joined at intervals by three nine metre long linking tunnels. The battery plotting room still stands, as do various other wartime structures such as the guardroom. But as Wanstone has reverted to being a working farm and permission should be sought before trying to visit. Alongside the main battery, Wanstone also contained a 3.7-inch AA battery and the whole complex was mined and alarmed to deter possible German commando-style raids.

The three initial batteries were later added to by 6-inch guns (defended by 40 mm Bofors anti-aircraft guns) at Lydden Spout, after three BL 13.5-inch Mk V naval guns from the First World War (named 'Gladiator', 'Scene Shifter' and 'Piece Maker') were brought out of retirement in 1939 and mounted on railway wagons. The resulting railway guns were operated by the Marines but moved by a team of Royal Engineers, and when not in use hidden in – among other places – Guston railway tunnel and Eythorne railway station on the East Kent Light Railway. The original Martin Mill railway was constructed and operated by Pearson & Son in 1897 for the construction of the Admiralty harbour. The line needed very little earth works until it reached the cliffs where terraces were cut into the cliff face down to the harbour and was in use until running into money problems in 1937.

Relaid in 1939, the line ran north of Fan Bay Battery, from there two new lines where laid east either side of the Dover to St Margaret's road, both terminating at St Margaret's.

The northern line supplied the 14-inch guns Winnie and Pooh and was also laid with two curved firing spurs for the 13.5-inch rail-mounted guns Gladiator, Scene Shifter and Piece Maker.

Similar in requirements to the German railway guns in that they had to be fired from a curved spur, the recoil was absorbed by special brakes acting on the wheels. Scene Shifter was later converted to an 18-inch Howitzer in November 1943. Maintenance was carried out near Lydden Spout.

The southern line had a curved firing spur close to Fan Bay The line then continued to Wanstone battery where two spurs where laid in front of the guns Clem and Jane for barrel changing: the barrels being transported by rail to Woolwich where they were re-lined. The line continued passing South Foreland Battery.

Diesel electric shunting locomotives, kept at the Martin Mill station yard, were used solely on the line as smoke from a steam locomotive might have given the guns positions away. The line was again lifted just after the end of the war. The British also had the 'Boche Buster', though that name should probably be attributed to the huge carriage the gun sat on rather than the gun itself. Utilised through the last year of the First World War as a 14-inch rail-mounted gun in France, the gun was pressed back into service in the early years of the Second World War, a sale to the Japanese having been scrapped. Mounted on a massive 18-inch howitzer carriage and manned by 11th Battery, 2nd Super Heavy Regiment, the weapon was based at the Bourne Park railway tunnel (part of the Elham Valley railway line that had been taken over by the military) and was intended to act as one of the final defences of the coastal area under threat of German invasion.

The British 'Boche Buster' railway gun.

Although by nature a rail-mounted gun of this type had a very limited traverse, it was possible to increase the arc of fire by adding loops and sidings to the main track and so enable Boche Buster to hit any German landing between Sandwich and Folkestone. The Bourne Park Tunnel enabled the weapon to be kept out of sight when not in action, and most wartime propaganda film and pictures show the gun near the southern portal. But, when called into action, it would have been moved to a designated spot that depended on the target. The bridge at Railway Hill in Barham had to be specially strengthened to take the weight of Boche Buster.

A hydro-pneumatic recoil system absorbed the force generated by firing and this let the gun move back approximately three feet, although the whole carriage would also have gone backwards down the track quite a distance. Boche Buster, in its WW2 configuration was mounted the Armstrong 18-inch Howitzer Mk I which slotted straight into the 14-inch mounting. Its 6 ft long shells, dispatched by a 260 lb cordite charge, still only had a range of around twelve miles but did weigh one and a quarter tons each. Along with it being a formidable weapon, the Boche Buster was also practical or effective in its manning. The gun would have been an easy target for a Stuka when out in the open had the *Luftwaffe* managed to gain air supremacy. Its role became increasingly one linked to propaganda purposes as the war dragged on.

Following D-Day, plans were initially made to ship the Boche Buster over to France but the gun offered nothing different from what the RAF could achieve with a deal less planning and consequently the Boche Buster vanished into obscurity.

Winnie and Pooh still had a role to play, however, and during September 1944, provided artillery cover for the 3rd Canadian Infantry Division which was tasked with capturing Calais and silencing the nearby German heavy batteries.

The gunnery duel, along with heavy bombing of the Dover and Folkestone areas, led to this stretch of the Channel being nicknamed Hellfire Corner and led to 216 civilian deaths, and damage to more than 10,000 homes and businesses. The long-distance confrontation only ceased when the Allies overran the German gun positions in the Pas de Calais in the second half of 1944. On the last day of shelling – 26 September 1944 – fifty shells landed in Dover, killing five people, the last of whom was

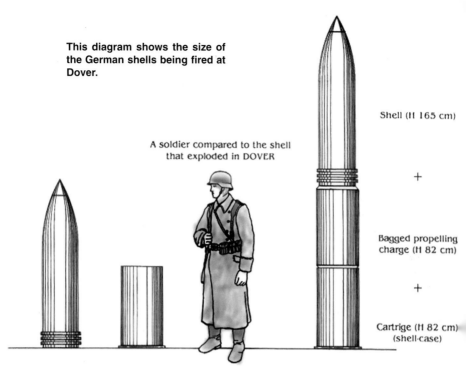

This diagram shows the size of the German shells being fired at Dover.

A soldier compared to the shell that exploded in DOVER

Shell (H 165 cm)

+

Bagged propelling charge (H 82 cm)

+

Cartrige (H 82 cm) (shell-case)

sixty-three-year-old Patience Ransley, killed by a shell from the Lindemann Battery at Sangatte whilst sheltering in the 270 metre long 'Barwick's Cave' cliff tunnel.

The following is an extract from *The Unlikely Death of Patience Ransley* by John Vaughan

The 26 of September 1944 was a day that was to be remembered by the residents of Dover, for it was on this day that their long ordeal at the hands of the German naval gunners in the batteries along the coast of France was to finally come to an end. Huge air raids had saturated the Nazi guns in the previous weeks, the British guns (the 14-inch 'Winnie' and 'Pooh' manned by the Royal Marines at St. Margaret's, and the 15-inch 'Jane' and 'Clem' manned by the Royal Artillery at Wanstone Farm) had kept up a steady counter-battery barrage in an attempt to suppress the German fire, and now Canadian troops were advancing to attack and silence the heavily fortified positions.

But the enemy were not yet defeated.

During the course of that terrible last day over fifty shells landed in the Dover area as the desperate gunners on the opposing shore, facing an uncertain future at the hands of the Canadian soldiers, followed orders and attempted to use up their remaining stocks of

ammunition against innocent civilians. Several deaths resulted in the town from this indiscriminate firing – houses collapsed into the streets pinning their unfortunate occupants in the rubble, a soldier died in a bungalow at Broadlees Road, a sailor died in Snargate Street when a pub was hit, an airman died in Frith Road, civilians died in their homes or out in the open. But surely the most unlikely and therefore most tragic death was that of sixty-three year old Patience Ransley... unlikely because she was sheltering deep underground, protected inside a tunnel lined with reinforced concrete and beneath 38 feet of chalk. This was the 900 foot long 'Barwick's Cave' shelter that ran from Snargate Street to Durham Hill.

There were many such deep shelters in Dover during the war and on this day they were all busy as the local populace sought cover from the ruthless bombardment above. They had every reason to feel safe and 'normal' life continued underground with conversations, playing cards, reading, knitting or just contemplative silence while the sound of distant explosions marked the arrival of yet another shell and the end of yet another property. But it was now that the bizarre, million-to-one incident occurred.

One of the 406 mm guns of Batterie Lindemann.

A one ton, 16-inch shell fired from Lindemann Battery, situated below the Noires Mottes escarpment near Sangatte, completed its curve high above the town and whistled down from the sky at a speed of 1,500 feet per second and an angle of 35 degrees. It penetrated a grave in the old cemetery above the shelter and bored its way down through a further twenty-four feet of solid chalk before exploding a mere seven feet above the thick reinforced concrete roof of the tunnel. The blast chamber formed by the explosion ruptured the roof over a length of twelve feet and poor Patience, sitting quietly in this spot, was killed instantly.

A few hours later the last of the German gun batteries had been silenced as nearly 30,000 Germans surrendered in the Pas de Calais area to the advancing Allies, and at last Dover was free from the almost daily bombardments that had terrorised the town and its people for five years.

'Winnie' British 14-inch coastal gun near Dover.

Chapter Two
ATTACK TO DEFENCE

FOLLOWING the Battle of Britain, during the latter stages of 1940 and the early months of 1941, it became obvious that the inability of the *Luftwaffe* to gain air supremacy over the RAF was always going to make an invasion of the British south coast a costly exercise, both in terms of men and time. There was also the the Royal Navy to consider.

Operation *Seelöwe* needed several key elements to fall into place before it could be sanctioned. The Royal Navy's presence had to be removed in possible landing areas from the Wash to the Thames and, most significantly along the Kent coast, while the *Luftwaffe* had to guarantee air supremacy over the RAF. The British submarine fleet also had to be largely neutralised. Most high-ranking German officers were sceptical this could ever be achieved, including *Reichmarschall* Hermann Göring, chief of the *Luftwaffe*, who wrote in a memorandum,

> *A combined operation having the objective of landing in England must be rejected. It could only be the final act of an already victorious war against Britain as otherwise the preconditions for success of a combined operation would not be met.*

Reichmarschall Hermann Göring.

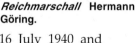

Hitler previously would not be deterred, however, issuing Directive No. 16 on 16 July 1940 and commenting:

> *As England, in spite of her hopeless military situation, still shows no signs of willingness to come to terms, I have decided to prepare, and if necessary to carry out, a landing operation against her. The aim of this operation is to eliminate the English Motherland as a base from which the war*

against Germany can be continued, and, if necessary, to occupy the country completely.

In reality, however, there was little enthusiasm for the invasion among Hitler's military hierarchy and little evidence that the *Heer*, *Kriegsmarine* and *Luftwaffe* ever seriously considered co-ordinating a joint plan to launch an invasion. Given the amount of time and planning needed to organise the Normandy landings four years later, the time frame the Germans were hoping to work to would clearly have been impossible.

Another insurmountable problem facing the *Kriegsmarine* was the almost complete lack of purpose-built landing craft that would have been required in a large-scale amphibious assault. They did possess the *Pionierlandungsboot 39*, a self-propelled, shallow-draft landing craft which could carry forty-five men and two vehicles or twenty tons of cargo. But by September 1940, only two were in service and navy chiefs recognized they would need a much larger vessel if they were to include tanks and heavy armour in an invasion force. Commercial barges were considered and more than 2,000 were requisitioned at one time from German rivers and the

Operation Seelöwe: plans for the invasion of England – a none starter without first defeating the Royal Air Force and the Royal Navy.

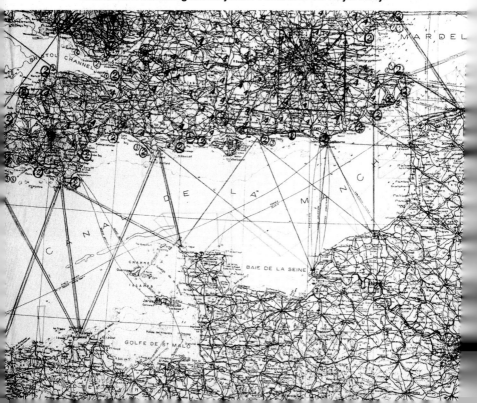

Converted canal barge with ramp.

A *Landswasserschlepper* (Land water tractor), one of seven pre-production models built by mid-1940 and followed by an order for fourteen more.

A rare photo of an ex-Czechoslovakian Army LTZ 38, taken into *Heer* service as the PzKfw 38(t) fitted with experimental flotation pontoons.

A PzKfw III Ausf. G, also known as a *Tauchpanzer* [diving or submerging tank], is undergoing wading trials in 1940. Note the air hose attached to the modified turret cupola.

Low Countries. But many of them had no engines and by the time the all-purpose *Marineprahmfähre* landing craft was developed in April 1941 the invasion of Britain had been abandoned as Hitler turned his attention towards the Soviet Union.

The decision to cancel Operation *Seelöwe* had, of course, left the Germans on the horns of a dilemma. They knew they had to protect the western flank of their acquired empire and were probably also aware that, at some time, an attack would come on *Festung Europa* if Britain and her Allies were allowed to regroup. No surprise then that a massive programme to install several lines of defence was initiated. Offshore, that meant minefields. The *Kriegsmarine* had been developing a marine mine research programme since the 1920s and were already mass producing several types at the beginning of the Second World War. These included contact and magnetic mines able to be laid by surface vessels, submarines and aircraft. By 1939, M1, M2 and bipolar M3 magnetic mines were already in use and by the end of the war, M4 mines were in full production. The latter being an improvement on the original M3. A derivation of the M1 (the M5) didn't prove a success, however, and never reached the factory floor while the KMA (*Küstenmine-A*), an explosive charge attached to a concrete base and placed in shallow water, went into production too late to have an impact on the Allied invasion fleet.

It took longer for the Germans to develop acoustic mines, largely due to the fact that they didn't expect their magnetic mines to have such an impact on British shipping. The British had invented the magnetic mine and the German High Command had simply assumed that they would already have counter-measures in place. When it became apparent they did not, further development on the acoustic mine was put on the back-burner with an authorised programme not being instigated until Dr Hell Firma developed the A1 for operational use in September 1940. Fields of moored contact mines were also common, especially around the major ports, though these were

Belgian Gates sited by the Germans as part of their Atlantic Wall defence system.

easier to negotiate and disable than the non-contact variety.

Closer to the shore, the *Cointet-élément* or Belgian Gate was a common obstacle. Made out of steel and positioned in relatively deep water so they would be fully hidden at high tide. Belgian

Belgian Gates being removed from a beach in 1944 by a Churchill AVRE.

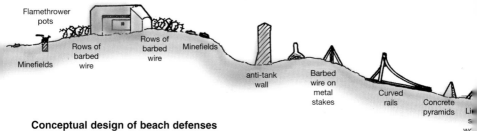

Flamethrower pots

Minefields

Rows of barbed wire

Rows of barbed wire

Minefields

anti-tank wall

Barbed wire on metal stakes

Curved rails

Concrete pyramids

Conceptual design of beach defenses

Gates looked exactly like a steel gate, only mounted on a flatbed made of concrete with four rollers on the bottom. The gate consisted of three sharply pointed 'spears' which were designed to pierce the hull of Allied landing craft and either strand or capsize its victim.

Further in, log ramps were commonly next in line. The ramps were generally built from one of two designs. The first consisted of two logs standing up straight, with one being longer than the other, while a third was placed on top of the two logs to create a slope. A *Tellermine* was then placed at the top of the sloping log.

The *Teller* 43 (plate) mine was mass-produced in Germany from 1943 until 1945. As its name suggests, it was a dinner plate-shaped circular mine with a central pressure plate that would detonate when a weight of more than 100kgs was applied. Generally used as an anti-tank device, it contained 5.5 kilograms of TNT and 3.6 million were thought to have been produced before the German surrender.

GERMAN TELLERMINE 43 (MUSHROOM)

7½ IN.

4 IN

SIDE FUZE WELL

12½ IN.

PRESSURE PLATE

BOTTOM FUZE WELL

CARRYING HANDLE

TOP VIEW

BOTTOM VIEW

The other principle design of log ramp was to have two short logs placed in an upside down V with a longer sloped log attached at the point of the V. Any Allied landing craft caught in the obstacle would ride up the slope of the log and detonate the mine at the top, causing untold damage to man and machine. The *Heer* had come up with a unique method of 'planting'

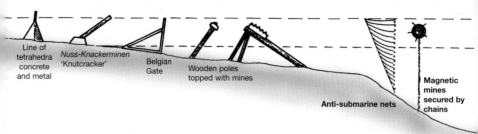

Line of tetrahedra concrete and metal

Nuss-Knackerminen 'Knutcracker'

Belgian Gate

Wooden poles topped with mines

Anti-submarine nets

Magnetic mines secured by chains

these log ramps by the end of 1943, using high-pressure hoses to create holes in the sand into which the contraption could be placed. The wet sand then closed around the base of the ramp, sealing it into position. It is estimated this method was nine times quicker than the normal method of pile-driving the logs into place.

Should the invading force survive that they were than confronted by the Czech Hedgehog. Approximately six feet high, hedgehogs were made of three steel rails riveted or welded into the shape of a tripod and normally weighted with concrete boots. Vulnerable beaches in France, particularly in the Pas de Calais, and Belgium had the highest density of hedgehogs as that was where the Germans though the Allies would land in the event of an invasion but getting them into place was a logistical nightmare. Resources were stretched by the time the mass deployment of hedgehogs was ordered and, with very few trucks assigned to

Cementing in a *Tschischer Igel* 'Czech Hedgehog' to give it greater stability. Named after the Czechoslovakian anti-tank defences deployed along the border with Germany but made redundant when Hitler occupied the territory after the Munich Agreement.

divisions along the Atlantic Wall, the obstacles had to be lifted on to horse-pulled carts and then man-handled down the beach. Considering their weight, it was a thankless task, especially as many of the troops involved were *Bodenständig* (lower-ranked infantrymen or conscripts) often not in the best of physical health. The hedgehogs were designed to pierce the hull of ships that came too close to the shoreline or to rip the hull off a less armoured landing craft. Usually laid out in shallower water, the hedgehogs' effectiveness was largely nullified on D-Day when the first wave of Allied forces came ashore at low tide which, of course exposed the position of the beach defences and allowed many landing craft to steer a course around them or deploy their load before arriving at the line. It did, of course, then provide an additional barrier for Allied troops on the beach, making them vulnerable to machine-gun fire and enfilade shelling while sappers and artillery crews devised a way to bridge anti-tank ditches and the *Eiserne Hemmkurven*, curved anti-tank ramps often made of corrugated iron. But it shouldn't be forgotten that cinema images of barbed-wire protected sand dunes weren't accurate at every landing beach in the Pas de Calais and Normandy and often the coastal road could be accessed once the sea wall had been crossed.

Minengranaten, artillery rounds hung over cliff edges and armed with an impact fuse, were also deployed on the bluffs surrounding the western edges of OMAHA Beach and I suppose one could also briefly mention 'Rommel's Asparagus', wooden logs driven into open fields along the French coastal plains in Normandy. Rommel encouraged their deployment and they were intended to prevent gliders and parachutes landing behind the Atlantic Wall fortifications but, as this is departing from the true subject matter of the book, I mention them only in passing.

Of course, Rommel's construction and mine-laying programme called for a very large expenditure of labour, and labour was scarce. Organization Todt was, by now, employed chiefly in the major port fortress areas, on V-weapon sites, and, in the spring of 1944, on railroad maintenance. In apportioning the remaining labour supply among the armies, the German *Fifteenth Army* received priority as most of élite troops of the German Forces on the Western front were contained within. The *Seventh Army*, therefore, struggled to complete its delegated defensive objectives. The *LXXXIVth Korps* was assigned three engineer battalions in January 1944, two for

Three defence items in this picture: Belgian Gates; post with a *Tellermine* atop, and the workers are carrying a section of railway track to construct a Czech Hedgehog.

bunker building and one for mine laying. In addition, 2,850 men of the former French Labour Service were set to work on a secondary defence line immediately behind the belt of coastal resistance points. Pleas for more construction hands were answered by attachments of two *Ostbataillone*. The *Ost* were volunteers recruited by the turncoat Russian General Vlassov from Soviet POWs, and conscripts largely from Eastern European countries including Armenia, Azerbaijan, Georgia and Turkmenistan. In Normandy, the *243.Infanterie Divisione* and *709.Infanterie Divisione* saw action after D-Day but their duties were usually confined to support roles such as construction and transport.

The only other available labour source were the combat troops. Increasingly, during 1944, infantrymen were employed in work details on the Atlantic Wall with consequent serious reduction of combat training. The reserve battalion of the *709th Division*, for instance, devoted three days a week exclusively to shoring up existing defences. The time for training in the rest of the week was further reduced by transport and guard details. During the first two weeks in May 1944, the infantry was employed full time deploying beach defences around the fishing port of Barfleur, on the eastern tip of the Cotentin Peninsula. The *709th* was an established division, but in 1944 it had a big influx of new recruits. A lack of adequate training meant that the combat fitness of the battalion steadily deteriorated, therefore, and worse still was the effect on the new and reorganized divisions that represented a large proportion of the German defending force in the west.

In the *Seventh Army*, all but one of the non-static infantry divisions were reorganized during 1944. New battalions accounted for six of the fourteen divisions under the army's command and all of these units were burdened with construction duties. In February Rommel, aware that coastal defences in Normandy and the Pas De Calais were totally incapable of repelling an Allied invasion, ordered that all available infantry in Northern France be utilised to lay mines and obstacles. On 25 May 25, the *Seventh Army* reported to the *Oberkommando des Heeres* (German Army High Command) which at that time was Hitler himself, that all its units were engaged in construction projects and that consequently the necessary training was not being carried out.

The only units exempt from construction work on the fortifications were the two parachute divisions. The *3.Fallschirmjäger Division* was brought into Brittany in March and stationed east of Brest. Its mission was to formulate plans for defence against airborne attack. The *5.Fallschirmjäger Division* moved into the Rennes area between the 5 and 14 of May with a similar mission. Both divisions were put under control of the *Second Parachute Korps* which, though answerable to the *Seventh Army*, was administratively and for training purposes under the *Third Air Force*. The *Luftwaffe* was solely responsible for parachute training and there was no structure in place for it to respond to any requests from the *Heer* for special dispensation.

As one can imagine, this frequently led to confrontation. *Reich Marshal* Göring ordered that the parachute divisions were not to be used for construction work, except when it was for their own benefit. The *5.Fallschirmjäger Division* hadn't even begun its training on D-Day, but the *3.Fallschirmjäger Division* proved one of the best prepared of the new units in *Seventh Army* and was to be heavily involved in the fighting.

At the time, Hitler seemed to accept that the lack of training for new recruits, under the circumstances, was a necessary price to pay to help shore up defences. Where Rommel's plans met with resistance was in his efforts to concentrate reserves nearer to the coast. The Germans had set their stall out to defend a fixed fortified line, therefore it followed that all forces not within striking distance of the Allied landings would be largely ineffective once a

bridgehead had been established. This deduction was the final extension of the doctrine of static defence implicit in the original decision to build the Atlantic Wall defences.

General Georg von Sodenstern, commanding the *Nineteenth Army*, wrote privately in the summer of 1943 of his fear that German High Command was becoming obsessed with the construction of huge masses of concrete.

As no man in his senses would put his head on an anvil over which the smith's hammer is swung, so no general should mass his troops at the point where the enemy is certain to bring the first powerful blow of his superior materiel.

General Georg von Sodenstern.

Rommel's response, in all likelihood, would have been that, firstly, there was no practical alternative and, secondly, that the Allied fire power would be initially limited on the beaches due to the very task of getting troops from sea to land. There was also the point that a German general in massing his troops in fortified positions was at least being offered some protection against the 'smith's hammer'.

The difference of opinion was essentially two opposing views of how a battle might progress. Rommel's chief of staff has testified that Rommel himself wanted the entirety of the forces at his disposal massed to repel an invasion, claiming the 'Desert Fox' could not envisage victory if the Germans were spread out defending a line with divisions kept in reserve. Rundstedt, like Sodenstern, was clearly more optimistic, perhaps because he had not had first-hand experience of the Allies' air power. In any case, he did not accept Rommel's prognosis and the influence of OB WEST was exerted spasmodically in resisting Rommel's efforts to shift the weight of the army forward to the coast, trying instead to free as many units as possible from the rigid defence system.

In practice any plan to introduce flexibility into the defence depended primarily on whether units could be made self-sufficient in combat. Many lacked mobility through lack of resources and often junior, inexperienced officers were left in charge. Through the early months of 1944, Rundstedt struggled to strengthen and provide some transport for the coastal divisions but it proved a near-impossible task. In the *Seventh Army* area, he did succeed in forming mobile *Kampfgruppen* (battle groups) from four of the infantry divisions (the 265th, 266th, 275th, and 353rd) defending the Brittany coast and, in case of a major invasion of Normandy, plans were in place to move these *Kampfgruppen* into the combat zone. On the Cotentin Peninsula, the 243rd Division was also converted from a static into a nominal attack infantry division. To facilitate this it was restructured with six infantry battalions. Four battalions were to be equipped with bicycles, while the artillery regiment, supply troops, and anti-tank battalion were to be motorized. The reorganization was scheduled to take place in late 1943 but the motorization planned to begin in May 1944 had little impact as, by that time, most vehicles had been requisitioned and moved north to the Pas de Calais, where it was anticipated the initial assault would materialize.

Even those vehicles that remained would hardly be associated

The two *Feldmarschälle,* Rommel and von Rundstedt could not agree on how the imminent Allied invasion should be repulsed.

Rommel, von Rundstedt, Gause and Zimmermann discuss strategy in Paris.

Ostbataillon **men manning an anti-aircraft gun in Normandy.**

with what now passes as transport in a modern army. For example, a mobile infantry unit in general was one equipped with bicycles, horse-drawn artillery and a mixture of horse and low-grade motor transport for supply purposes. The nomenclature mobile referred more to its ability to maintain itself in the field than because of any claim to move rapidly from one place to another.

For the most part, the Germans lacked the resources even to provide that limited mobility for the divisions tasked with defence of the Atlantic Wall and von Rundstedt's efforts to restore mobility to his static divisions was, on the whole, an abject failure. By the beginning of May 1944, largely as a result of the Allies' successful attacks on German and French railways, the *Seventh Army* had already resorted to using anything and everything on wheels to form corps transport companies.

Rundstedt's vain efforts to mobilize his army continued to be hampered Rommel's determination to dig in every available soldier and gun along the coast line, however. After an inspection trip in the *LXXXIV Corps* sector in Normandy in February, Rommel had concluded that reserves were being held in too many numbers too far from the coast. In particular, he felt that the *352nd Division*, located near St. Lo, and the *243.Division*, held near la Haye du Puits, should be regrouped so that they could be committed in the first hours after an enemy landing.

Seventh Army headquarters therefore ordered that the divisional reserves of the *709* and *716 Divisions* (the foreign conscripts of the *795.Georgian Bataillon* and *642.Ostbataillon* respectively) should be fully committed to coastal defence, while the *243* and *352 Divisions* should be moved to the north. The *352.Artillerie Regiment* was told to dig in and reinforce emplacements in perceived vulnerable areas along the coast and placed under the control of the *716.Division*.

Similar reshuffling in Brittany put the artillery of the *275* and *353 Divisions* into static defence positions, with the *352.Division* brought out of reserve to add to their numbers. On the approval of OB WEST, all of these changes were accomplished by the 19th March, 1944 and meant that only the one full regiment, the *352.Division*, plus the *Füsilierbataillon* were held in corps reserve at Bayeux.

At this point Hitler was having serious misgivings about the strategy of his generals, however, and was considering whether all units of limited mobility located immediately behind the coast shouldn't, as a matter of policy, be incorporated in the first line of resistance, leaving only fully mobile forces as reserves inland. However, as General Jodl pointed out, except for three divisions, all units were already far enough forward for their artillery to have an impact on possible areas of invasion. Jodl maintained that to advance all troops into the coastal fortifications could be counter-productive since it was already known that newer concrete bunkers offered limited shelter and Allied bombers were capable of

A Panzer IV in the Caen area prior to the invasion. Note that much of the Schürzen hull side skirting has been lost.

inflicting massive damage on field defences if their positions were exposed. In Brittany and on the Cotentin peninsula, it would also be imperative troops were held behind the coastal defences in order to resist probable airborne landings.

A wholesale commitment of all forces to coastal defence was, therefore, ruled impractical, but Rommel continued his push to shift the weight of his army westwards. In April, the *21st Panzer Division* was moved from Rennes to the strategically vital inland port of Caen and its battalions positioned on opposite banks of the Orne River. The artillery section was sent to support existing defences near Ouistreham on the coast. The other two Panzer divisions directly under Rommel's command were sent to reinforce the *Fifteenth Army*, one between Rouen and Paris, the other near Amiens. In May, another inspection tour convinced Rommel that movement of units from right to left into the invasion area would be impossible. He therefore requested that the four more divisions in reserve be moved nearer the coast. Rundstedt, of course, protested and got his own way – Rommel's influence, it appears, was already on the wane.

These four divisions, therefore, were the only mobile units in the west on the eve of the invasion which could be specifically designated strategic reserves. Three were located within a few hours drive of the Normandy battlefields, but the fourth was on the Belgium-Netherlands border and effectively out of the equation come D-Day.

The dispute between Rommel and Rundstedt was never resolved and it undoubtedly hampered the Germans in the hours after D-Day. A compromise could have seen more structured opposition to the Allies after 6 June but the pool of mobile reserves had shrunk below what was needed for an effective counter-attack and had been divided among three centres of commands, which further diluted its effectiveness. A command to launch a counter-attack was almost impossible to obtain therefore and, though considerable forces were still available on the road to Paris, they would be unable to reach the battlefield in time to prevent a successful invasion.

The scene was set for the war in Europe to take a decisive turn.

Chapter Three

THE ORGANISATION TODT

INSIDE FIVE YEARS, according to a 1945 British Intelligence report, the Organisation Todt carried out the most impressive development and construction programme since the halcyon days of the Roman Empire.

More than 1,400,000 men built bunkers, roads, blockhouses and bridges for the *Wehrmacht* but, though they wore predominantly black uniforms with swastika armbands, the majority of their number were neither soldiers nor members of a party organisation. Almost uniquely a Nazi body independent of party control, the Organisation Todt was the only organisation in the Third Reich, besides the Hitler Youth, to be allowed to bear the name of a member of the party elite. Ideally placed to garner the fruits of Hitler's expansionism without carrying the stigma of what the Nazis stood for, the reactions it name provoked could vary from adoration to fear but it was still a remarkable product of one young engineer's vision.

Fritz Todt was born in Pforzheim, on the edge of the Black Forest, on 4 September 1891. His father owned a small factory in a town renowned for its precision engineering industries which included watch-making and jewellery setting. As a young man Todt studied engineering at Karlsruhe before enrolling at the Technical College in Munich.

The First World War was to bring a temporary halt to Todt's education but he was to distinguish himself on the battlefield, winning the Iron Cross while attached to the infantry and later earning a mention in dispatches as an observer in the embryonic *Luftwaffe*. Following the cessation of hostilities, he returned to Munich to finish his studies before starting work with Grun & Bilfinger AG Mannheim, moving on to civil engineers Sager & Woerner in 1921.

The defining moment in Todt's life arguably came a year later when he decided the ideology of the new Nazi party was closest to his way of thinking. Rising quickly through the ranks, Fritz Todt was promoted to *Oberführer* (a rank roughly equivalent to a

Brigadier General) in 1931. It was also around this time that he completed his doctorate *Fehlerquellen bei der Konstruktion von Asphalt und Asphaltdeckschichten*, which translates as, 'Sources of defect in the construction of tarmac and asphalt road surfaces'. Two years later Hitler appointed him Inspector General of German Roadways and, following his supervision of Germany's still impressive *Autobahn* network, he was promoted again to General Commissioner for the Regulation of the Construction Industry in 1935 and given the military rank of *Generalmajor* in the *Luftwaffe*. Todt's vision and engineering expertise hadn't gone unnoticed abroad and in 1936 he was awarded a Nobel Prize for Science, though Hitler was to forbid his acceptance. Two years later, Organisation Todt was born.

In 1938 Todt, by now indisputably Hitler's chief architect and engineer, had been commissioned to complete the building of the West Wall on the German–French border without delay. To do this he brought in the gangs he had used to complete his newly-built *autobahn* system. Further, he had the authority to mobilize the RAD.

The RAD (*Reichsarbeitsdienst Männer*) were groups of civilian workers, often between 1,200- and 1,800-strong, who could be called upon to serve the state in times of need. They were equipped only with a spade and a bicycle but would often be ferried to where they were needed by those members of their party who had access to a truck or car. Between 1938 and 1940, 1.75 million Germans were

Men of a labour battalion learning to march. Conscription into the RAD served as an introduction to military service as it was organised on military lines – note the polished, spotless, shovels.

The RAD (*Reichsarbeitsdienst*) organized like a military unit and marching to their own song.

conscripted into the RAD and the gangs were a familiar sight at the roadside, gathered together in the early morning light awaiting transport, their highly-polished shovels shouldered like guns. Most work parties had a political activist attached to remind them they were working for the good of Germany. Some would even have 'troublemakers' inserted to root out possible resistance to the Nazi doctrine. The RAD was, after all, regarded as a valuable tool in the indoctrination of the masses.

Throughout the war, sabotaging any form of engineering project was punishable by death which acted as a particular deterrent to 'guest workers' (*Gastarbeitnehmer*), prisoners of war, concentration camp internees and civilian 'volunteers' who were used in increasing numbers after 1940. From 1942 until May 1945, it is estimated that Organisation Todt employed 1.4 million labourers on projects directly connected to the war effort. Only one per cent were Germans, often those rejected for military service. Around the same amount was forced labour from concentration camps with the remainder prisoners of war or civilians from conquered countries. Whatever their nationality, all were treated as slaves. Most did not survive the war.

47

Admiral Dönetz inspects the construction work of the RAD on the Atlantic Wall.

In the latter stages of the Second World War, the RAD developed into an almost exclusively military faction, manning anti-aircraft guns and seeing action on the Eastern front as well as being used on the frontline as the Allies advanced across Europe in 1945.

Todt also used the *Heer* construction battalions to build his defences, placing his trust in the principles of private enterprise, the art of innovation, and the triumph of technical rationale over bureaucracy. Under Todt's supervision in 1938-39, almost half a million workers constructed concrete bunkers on a scale that had never before been contemplated, leaving the military to plan its invasion of Poland without the need to worry about interference from the French.

Following the outbreak of war Todt, as a close *confidante* of the Führer, was given an ever increasing number of construction tasks vital to the war effort. The Organisation Todt followed the conquering *Heer* across Europe, repairing bridges, dams, road systems, and bombed factories, and in the process playing a large role in exploiting the occupied countries.

In the Balkans, it was responsible for the mining of ores essential to the German war effort and their shipment to key manufacturing sites in the Ruhr valley; and the roads on which Hitler's divisions marched to Yugoslavia and Greece were upgraded. In the west building gangs, often including local forced labour, were put to work from Norway to the Bay of Biscay via the Channel Islands to construct the Atlantic Wall. The great U-boat pens in St Nazaire and the construction of airfields used in the bombardment of Allied convoys to Murmansk were also the work of Organisation Todt as, later, were the launching ramps for the V-1 'doodle bug'.

After February 1940, when Fritz Todt became minister for weapons and munitions, he was given ever more responsibility for the war economy. The Organisation Todt expanded in consequence, recruiting large numbers of foreign workers. It was, however, attracting fewer Germans with most able-bodied men being conscripted into military service. Those employed after the summer of 1940 had an average age of fifty-three.

A huge percentage of the Organisation Todt's members were young non-Germans, however, with many of those who volunteered signing contracts they didn't understand. But most foreign workers had no choice but to accept the terms of their employment. They were either slave labour, drafted in from concentration camps, or prisoners of war. They would be forced to work long hours on meagre rations and often had to sleep on the building sites themselves, under the close supervision of the SS.

In June 1941, as Hitler ordered the invasion of the USSR, it was soon realised that German military construction battalions alone were not capable of providing the necessary engineering support required to ensure Operation BARBAROSSA didn't stall.

Armband.

It was probably at this point that the Organisation Todt became an integral part of the Nazi machine, though its founder remained adamant that his organization wasn't made an official arm of the Third Reich. Todt still had one eye on the future and thought that a closer affiliation to either the party or the armed forces would reflect badly on his

Entrance to the *Wolfschanze*, (Wolf's Lair), Hitler's field HQ located in a forest near Rastenburg, Germany.

organisation if Germany was to lose the war.

Whether this stubborn refusal to be totally immersed in the German hierarchy was directly connected to Fritz Todt's mysterious death in February 1942, nobody knows or can prove. But there was more than a suggestion of skulduggery. Todt was being flown back to Berlin from a meeting with Hitler at his Wolf's Lair at Rastenburg (now in Poland); ironically, Todt had designed this complex and supervised its construction. He'd reportedly had a heated discussion with the Führer over the prospects of success on the Eastern Front without a more defined infrastructure.

His Junkers 52 exploded in a fireball shortly after take-off; he was aged fifty.

Fritz Todt was buried with full military honours in Berlin and became the first recipient, albeit posthumously, of the new German Order (*Deutscher Orden*). On the day of his funeral, Britain's Foreign Broadcast Monitoring Service recorded the following from the Federal Communications Commission (some of the text had to be assumed due to poor radio reception). It not only eulogised Todt's contribution to the Nazi war machine but it also gave an insight into the thinking at that time as regards objectives;

50

In this sad hour, it is very hard for me to think of a man whose deeds speak louder and more impressively than words can do. When we received the terrible news of the misfortune, to which our dear Master Builder Dr. Todt had fallen victim, many million Germans had the same feeling of emptiness which always occurs when an irreplaceable man is taken from his fellow men.

The whole German nation knows that the death of this man means an irreplaceable loss for us. It is not only the creative personality which was taken from us, but it is also the loyal man and unforgettable comrade, whose departure touches us so deeply.

Dr. Todt was a National Socialist. He was that not only intellectually, but also with his whole heart. The first contact with the Party was in the year 1922, the first encounter with me personally had not only drawn this man inwardly to me, but also bound him outwardly to adhere to what he envisioned as the only possibility for a German renaissance.

The combination of the national concept with the social concept did not appear to this technician and engineer, who at one time depended for his living on the labour of his own hands, as a problem to be solved or even as a question to be answered, but as the categorical obligation of the struggle for a real German re-arming, which had to be more than just a mere restoration of an external form of government.

As early as 1922 this man saw clearly that the aim of a German revival had to be, not a restoration of shattered old forms, but a revolution of the German spirit, of German thought, and hence of the German people in its inner social order.

In 1919 he completed his studies and in the winter of 1920 passed his final examination at the School for Advanced Technical Studies in Munich. It is interesting to note that the subject of his doctor's thesis at the School for Advanced Technical Studies in Munich is the

51

Hitler places the German Order on Todt's funeral pillow.

following: "*Disadvantages of Highway Construction using Tar and Asphalt.*"

On the 5 of January 1923, Dr. Engineer Fritz Todt of Pforzheim finally joined the National Socialists, namely in the local troop at Oetting in Bavaria. Immediately after the ban against the Party was lifted in November 1923, he became a full member and remained one until January 1925. In the meantime he was unswervingly active in the Party after various charges against him were finally quashed.

In 1931, he joined the S.A. (Storm-Troopers) and to assert himself as a real National Socialist, began as a lowly trooper. He then becomes a squad leader and in the same year he advanced to standard bearer. By 1938, he had risen to Chief Leader, Brigade Leader, and finally Chief Brigade Leader. Only his activity in the Party is not all expended in the service of the Storm Troopers. In the beginning he was an associate of the Progressive League of German Architects and Engineers in Munich and, in addition, is Technical Consultant of highway construction in the then existent office for Economic coordination and Work Procurement of the N.S.D.A.P. (the National Socialist German Workers Party.) In 1932, he had already amalgamated the Construction Engineers and Countrymen League and the Progressive League of German Architects and Engineers with the Technical Bureau, resulting in the National Socialist German Technical Union under his leadership.

52

In 1936 the Technical Bureau was raised to the Central Technical Bureau in recognition of its meritorious service. In the meantime. Dr Todt entered that field of activity, where for the first time not only the German people but in addition a large part of the rest of the world was to become acquainted with him. In connection with the opening of the Automobile Exposition, which took place in 1933, I tried to realize the principles proclaimed at that time in the field, not only of the improvement of the German road network already in existence, but also in the field of the construction of new special auto roads. This was a general plan which essentially only embraced the general principles. In Dr. Todt, after long trials and deliberations, I believed I had found a man who was suited to transform a theoretical intention into practical reality. A brochure published by him about new ways of road construction was submitted to me and especially strengthened me in this hope.

After long discussions I entrusted him, on 30 June 1933, with the task of building the new Reich's auto roads, and in connection with this, the general reform of the whole German highway construction system, as general director of construction for the German highway construction system. With that, this man had found a frame which he began to fill in a truly incomparable and imperishable way.

The German Reich's auto roads are, in the planning of their layout and the execution, the work of this quite unique technical and artistically talented man. We can no longer think of the German Reich without these roads. In the future also they will find their continuation as natural great communication lines in the whole European transportation region. But what has in addition been done in Germany in this same time in the broadening and improvement of roads, in the elimination of bad curves, in the construction of bridges is so incomprehensible in its scope, that only an exhaustive study will permit a comprehensive and just conception of the accomplishment in its entirety.

Thus, it was only natural that this man was appointed chief administrator, first, for the regulation of all construction, and that then, in the Four Year Plan, he was given a special position as Inspector General for special projects.

Meanwhile, the clouds of a more and more menacing war danger began to gather about Germany at that time already. When it could no longer be ignored, especially as a result of the unswervingly inciting speeches of Churchill and his following in England, that in view of the uncertain situation of the parliamentary democrats in those countries there might be a sad change of regime working against peace, I was obliged to make provision for the defense of the Reich on a large scale and as soon as possible.

I had conceived the plan of erecting a fortification opposite the Maginot Line, but from different points of view, which was to protect the vitally important western portion of the Reich against any attack, under any circumstances, even in the event that quite large German forces ... in the East. There was only one man who was in a position to solve this technical engineering problem, unique in the history of the world, and to solve it, indeed, in the shortest possible time.

When, on 28 May 1938, I made known my resolve to the army and the air force, I entrusted the Inspector General for Construction, Dr. Todt, at the same time with the responsibility and supervision of the construction of the largest part by far of this gigantic new work, in cooperation with the proper military authorities, with the provision that as early as September 1938, at the latest, at least 5,000 concrete and steel positions would have to be ready or usable.

The war which broke out presented new... problems to this greatest organizer of modern times. A system of great roads for deploying troops had to be built up in those regions of the Reich in the shortest possible time, which previously had been very much neglected. Thousands and more thousands of kilometres of roads were either newly built or widened, provided with a hard surface and made dust proof. When the fighting finally began, units called into being by this unique talent for organization marched behind and forward with the troops, removed obstacles, rebuilt destroyed bridges, improved roads, erected everywhere new bridges over valleys, ravines, rivers and canals, and thus complemented in an indispensable way the engineering troops who were actively fighting. The victory in Norway, the victory in the West brought new tasks. After former party comrade Todt had been named to the Reich's Ministership for Armaments and Munitions, and thereby had to organize and lead a new, truly formidable sphere, there came in addition the task of protecting German sovereign territory against enemy attacks through the construction of new, powerful fortifications.

His work, including his service as Reich's Minister for Armaments and Munitions, this man accomplished with a minimum of assistance. He was without doubt in this field the greatest organizer whom Germany, whom the German people, has

A section of Germany's autobahn shortly after completion. The motorway network is one of the Todt Organisation's lasting legacies.

produced up to now. He managed with the smallest conceivable staff of his own, and without any bureaucracy, to utilize all the agencies and forces which appeared useful towards the solution of his problems.

Much of what the man has done can be made known to the German people or brought to the amazed attention of the world, only after the war. What this man has created is so unique that we all can not thank him enough for it.

If, however, I spoke just now about the technician and organizer, Fritz Todt, I must also bear in mind the man, who has stood so near to us all. It is not possible to give any better characterization of his personality than in determining that this great director of work never has had an enemy either in the movement or among his co-workers.

There was a time when fate forced him, the greatest construction engineer of all times, to earn his daily bread as a simple labourer, just as this has happened in my own case. Never for a moment was he ashamed of that fact. On the contrary, in later years it was for him a source of proud and satisfying memories, when he, the greatest construction chief the world has ever known, had occasion to look at or to show to others a photograph of himself depicting him in his

55

sober working attire, working on the road, covered with dust and dirt, or in front of a seething vat of tar. For this reason he especially took to his heart his German "road builders," as he called them.

It was his continuous desire to improve their social and often so trying living conditions, to replace their former miserable tents with modern... and shelters, to take away from the road worker's camps the character of stagnant mass quarters, and especially to create within the labourer the feeling that road building, yes, the entire field of construction is a field of work of which anyone can always be proud, because it creates documents not only of the highest importance to mankind, but also of the greatest durability.

Before Dr. Todt the work of the road worker was not regarded very highly. Today the 10,000 road builders are a proud fraternity fully aware of their great usefulness. In this way be has accomplished a basic national socialistic educational work, and for this we are today especially indebted to him. Just as every human progress has had its model, so the Organization Todt has created permanent social models and is on its way to develop them still further.

Gradually not only a social injustice, but also a human, thoughtless folly, was to be eliminated, and eliminated, indeed, forever.

Thus, whether this man had dealings with a working man, a Minister or a general, he always remained the same. An equally confident leader and solicitous friend of all decent national comrades. It was no wonder that this man, who so loved his people, was passionately attached to his family, his wife and his children. The creator of the greatest technical enterprises spent every free hour, whenever he could, among the great creations of Nature, in the little house beside the lake, in the midst of his beloved Bavarian peasants.

When under the fire of enemy guns the West Wall was completed, while in Poland the columns of the Organization Todt for the first time joined the advancing armies and gave them assured supply lines, I had it in my mind to award him the Knight's Cross, as one of the leading creators of German resistance. However, I changed my mind.

Because this distinction, famous though it is, could never have done justice to the importance of this unique man. I had already made the decision, some time previously, to establish such a decoration, which, founded on the principles of our movement, is to honour, in several classes, the most valuable services that a German can perform for his people.

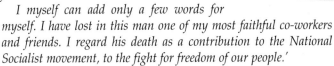

After the conclusion of the campaign against France, I said to Dr. Todt that I proposed for him some day, as God wills the recognition of his unique service, that he will be the first to whom I shall award the highest class of the order. In his modesty at that time he did not want to know anything about it. So now today I confer for the first time, in the name of the German people and its National Socialist movement, the new order on our dear and unforgettable party comrade, Dr. Todt, the general inspector of our roads and builder of the West Wall, the organizer of armaments and munitions in the greatest battle of our people for their freedom and their future.

I myself can add only a few words for myself. I have lost in this man one of my most faithful co-workers and friends. I regard his death as a contribution to the National Socialist movement, to the fight for freedom of our people.'

Whatever, if any, Hitler's role in Todt's demise, such public praise from the Nazi Party leader was rare and Albert Speer faced no easy task in stepping into his boots as head of the Organisation Todt. Speer had no master plan: he merely continued the policies initiated by his predecessor, though he did contribute greatly to the co-ordination of industries crucial to the war effort and had a sufficient sense of self-preservation to ensure all future plans were endorsed by Hitler himself. Speer had one big advantage over possible rivals in securing the personal backing of the Nazi dictator; he was able to bypass Germany's military leaders and largely ignore the Nazi government's much-maligned 'Four Year Plan', directly agreeing policy with Hitler in regular 'Führer Conferences' held between the two men until 1944.

Speer was responsible for important administrative changes to improve war output. In April 1942 he had set up Central Planning, an executive board under his direction which decided on the allocation and distribution of raw materials and essential equipment on a national scale. He also set up an interlocking system of production committees for all crucial weaponry, each committee being responsible for all the firms involved in the production of a particular weapon group.

The main committees became the focal point for planning and supervision of all military output, and the system led to massive improvements in efficiency, co-operation and, eventually, centralized control.

Speer was also successful politically, pushing the armed forces out of their role in the war economy and reducing the level of military interference in industrial matters. At the same time he insisted on bringing industrialists and engineers into the war apparatus so that industrial production of was handled by the experts who had experience of attainble output targets. The principle of 'industrial self-responsibility', as Speer called it, was to bring Germany rich dividends. In two years, and despite the effects of the Allied strategic air offensive, armaments production trebled and the output of military aircraft increased almost fourfold, the figures leaping from 11,000 to 39,000. Only intensive bombing from the summer of 1944 brought a gradual decline, leading to a sharp collapse as the Allies advanced on Berlin in the early months of 1945.

Long before that, however, Speer's influence had been on the wane. By 1944, he no longer enjoyed the complete backing of Hitler and the SS had been able to gain a greater say in running war production. Speer was officially in charge of aircraft production in 1944, though he needed the co-operation of Erhard Milch and no longer controlled labour supply, one of the critical limiting factors for the war economy. Hitler placed this under Fritz Sauckel, who refused to co-ordinate his plans with Speer's strategy for raw materials and industrial rationalization.

The intensive bombing of Germany finally destroyed the rationalization plans by forcing the de-centralization of production, disrupting the delicate infrastructure of distribution and sub-contracting set up by the committee system. When Hitler wanted to shift all production underground, Speer proved reticent. When the SS promised to complete the programme instead, this caused the rapid erosion of Speer's standing and the rise of new SS economic leaders, Xavier Dorsch and Hans Kammler. By the end of the war, Speer was disillusioned with Hitler. He refused to implement his

Albert Speer takes on the job.
A Todt overseer keeps an eye on some slave labourers.

orders for a scorched earth policy as German forces retreated further into the Fatherland, leaving much of Germany's new military industries to help with the post-war economic revival.

At no time did the authorities succeed in welding the military and civilian construction units together. The Organisation Todt remained relatively independent, even when, in the autumn of 1944, it was renamed the Front-Organisation Todt. Those of its members who could be trusted were armed, and told to report to authorities to help in the defence of the Germany. Many of the structures it had created had been destroyed by this time and, after the German defeat, the Organisation Todt itself was disbanded and placed on a blacklist.

Speer, as its last recorded leader when the war ended, was convicted at the Nuremberg trials of encouraging forced recruitment and employing slave labour. He was sentenced to twenty years in prison. Large parts of the Atlantic Wall remain as a monument to Todt's ingenuity, however, and his role in the days when Germany threatened to rule Europe should not be underestimated.

Chapter Four

CONSTRUCTION OF THE
ATLANTIC WALL BUNKERS

D ESIGN PLANS were meant to be rigidly followed, but it is estimated that less than half of the casemates, bunkers and shelters that comprise the Atlantic Wall in France did not strictly adhere to the blueprints laid down by the architects and engineers of the *Festungspionier Korps* (Fortress Engineering Corps). Fluctuations in terrain accounted for most deviations, particularly in the actual location of the various components of a battery or strongpoint. The shortage of essential materials also caused builders to compromise on the designated quality of bunkers as the war progressed. But, that said, the various types of concrete defences remaining to this day are, by and large, still recognisable as to the purpose for which they were intended.

Tobruk or *ringstand* (*Ringstände*) are among the most prolific as they were incorporated into virtually every

A *Tobrukstand* or *Ringstände*.

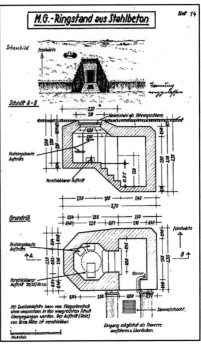

61

fortification that could support them, including kitchens, stores and wash houses, while the R621 personnel bunker (*Gruppenstand*), and associated R501 are also numerous as are the H667 and H677. However, the most recognisable structure are the sturm or reinforced casemates prevalent in the large shore batteries. The photograph of a German soldier stood alongside one of the massive

guns of the *Batterie Lindemann* in the Pas de Calais enclosed in its three metre thick casemate is one of the iconic images of the Second World War and one used frequently by Nazi propagandists to convince both the German people and possible invaders that the Atlantic Wall was an impregnable barrier. But the true situation was that there remained many long-range guns, particularly those under the control of the army, and their crews on the Atlantic Wall, particularly

Propaganda image portraying the invincibility of the Atlantic Wall.

around the landing beaches, that had minimal protection from attack on D-Day.

The *Festung* (fortress) ports, Calais and Boulogne in the Pas de Calais, and Cherbourg, Le Havre and Dieppe in Normandy, were heavily fortified but the stretches of the Atlantic Wall in what were perceived as less strategically-vital areas were still a work in progress in the early months of 1944. The timeline for the construction of many casemates proves the point perfectly. Of the original brief to build 15,000 entirely encased bunkers by the summer of 1944, Organisation Todt had completed almost two thirds by D-Day. Unfortunately for Germany, work on those in Lower Normandy was running approximately seven weeks behind construction in the area around Calais and Boulogne, where Hitler had been led to believe the invasion would take place.

From 1937, plans for all buildings and emplacements in German field batteries were subject to standardisation and allocated design numbers in keeping with their aspect, purpose and the branch of the armed forces responsible for their operation. In simple terms, a gun emplacement with the prefix OB (*Offene Bettung*) meant that it was open to the elements while Vf (*Verstärktfeldmässig*) indicated a reinforced position. If a bunker design number was preceded by the letter H, it indicated that the army (*Heer*) oversaw its administration. An L (*Luftwaffe*) pointed to an air force bunker while an M meant the navy (*Kriegsmarine*) had control. Occasionally, more advanced fortifications were given a SK suffix indicating special design (*Sonderkonstruktion*); but standardised bunkers commonly had the prefix R (*Regelbau*) attached. Thus a Vf 600 could be recognised as a fortified gun emplacement, an H667 an anti-tank gun casemate operated by the army and an R501 a standard construction defendable command bunker and so forth. For further clarification, a glossary is included at the beginning of this book.

It's probably fair to say that serious construction of the Atlantic Wall didn't really begin until the summer of 1942. There was once a theory that the ill-fated raid on Dieppe, which took place on 17 August 1942, was the catalyst which persuaded the Germans to begin fortifying the Western Front to a much greater degree but, in fact, Hitler had already issued a directive (Directive No. 40) in March of that year to lay the groundwork for the massive construction programme which would compliment the already established Westwall on Germany's border with France. British

The ill-fated raid on Dieppe. Note the ventilation pipes for deep wading on the Churchill tanks.

commando raids, including one which caused substantial damage to the dry docks in St Nazaire, were highlighting weaknesses in defence along the French coast and the Dieppe fiasco occurred four days after Hitler had met Albert Speer, the new head of the Todt Organisation, and senior engineers to finalise building plans. The raid on Dieppe proved a dark point in history for the Allies but without the sacrifice of the British and Canadian forces involved, the Normandy landings may never have succeeded.

Operation JUBILEE was the first ever attempt to land tanks in an amphibious assault but it was doomed to failure from the start. Though Royal Navy destroyers had laid down a barrage and five squadrons of Hurricanes had strafed defences, the British No. 4 Commando success in nullifying the western coastal battery overlooking the port was the only successful aspect of the mission.

No. 3 Commando's landing craft were attacked by a German patrol with the result that they lacked the firepower to complete their objective on the eastern edge of the proposed landing area yet still the main attack force comprising the 14th Canadian Tank Battalion (Calgary Regiment), Royal Marine A Commando, the Essex Scottish Regiment, Mont-Royal Fusiliers and the Royal Hamilton Light Infantry continued on to the beaches of Dieppe while the Royal Regiment of Canada, the South Saskatchewan Regiment and the Cameron Highlanders moved on outlying targets.

Canadian casualties were unacceptably high at Dieppe.

The Churchill tanks could not break through the anti-tank defences.

But, of course, the advantage of surprise had been lost and, though Dieppe wasn't as heavily defended as other fortified ports, the Germans were still well prepared. Communication immediately broke down between the assault force and its Royal Navy escort as well as the two commando forces meant to be guarding their flanks. The majority of the Canadian Churchill tanks couldn't get off the beaches because of tank traps and the sea walls in front of them and they could not get a grip in the unstable shingle. Those that scrambled on to solid ground were met by an anti-tank brigade that had been hurried to the coast by Dieppe's *Hafenkommandant* (port commander).

The Canadians, for whom this was their first taste of combat in Europe, were particularly hard hit. The first few waves of troops who made it on to the beach were cut down by enfilade fire from machine-guns. Scattered infantry did manage to infiltrate the town but most were destined to be among the 4,000 Canadian and British troops killed, wounded or captured by German forces in Dieppe.

It was a harsh lesson but one that the Allies put to good use two years later. It was obvious the outright storming of a major French port could never succeed and the army, navy and air forces of the invasion forces also understood that the need for reliable intelligence and communication was paramount. The inability of the Churchill tanks to get past beach defences further highlighted the need for the development of more adaptable armour to protect a beachhead. Operation JUBILEE contributed to German arrogance over the capability of the Atlantic Wall. Prior to 1942, apart from the main ports, only the Channel Islands which, for some reason, Hitler did not want to risk falling back into British hands, had been heavily fortified. Coastal artillery on mainland France, therefore, was almost exclusively housed in kettle gun emplacements prior to that date.

The level of fortification on and around the D-Day beaches varied between the heavily fortified *Festunghäfe* ports and ordinary field entrenchments. While the defences on the coast of Lower Normandy (the Cote De Nacre) did have a significant number of concrete defences, the most common types were small, open tobruks and gun pits, not the fully enclosed bunkers utilised in coastal batteries.

CONSTRUCTION

Atlantic Wall bunkers were uniformly made from reinforced concrete, though construction quality suffered badly as the war progressed. After a site for a fortification had been surveyed and the ground levelled to specification, the floor was poured from concrete. In 1942, the aggregate, sand and cement were imported from as far afield as Poland and Eastern Germany but by 1944, sand was being dug from the beaches of the French coast and instead of stone-rich aggregate, sea-shell fragments were being added to the mixture. On top of a lack of basic ingredients at this time, it was not unknown for local forced labour to sabotage the concrete mixture with sugar, etc, supplied by partisans, though it meant summary execution for anyone caught in the act.

The wooden moulds for the interior were constructed from beams and planks, and the reinforced concrete built up around them. Steel reinforcing bars (rebars) were spaced 25 cm apart, putting about 50 kg of steel into every cubic meter of bunker wall. Anything that had to be anchored into the concrete was put into place at the same time. Steel armour plates, firing ports, ventilation

Todt workers dig out the ground to house the casemate.

Shuttering is prepared prior to the pouring of concrete for the construction of these underground shelters.

shafts and stove chimneys for example.

If the bunker was designed to have an emergency exit, as the R501 did, then that would be built in brick and surrounded by a thin layer of concrete. As the emergency formed part of the bunker's outer wall, this would be installed at this time.

The inside of the roof was also built together with the interior fittings, by placing steel I-beams at regular intervals across the narrower dimension of the room for maximum strength and

Cement mixers about to pour a load into the shuttering.

A casemate nearing completion.

putting steel plates between them. Occasionally wooden planks were used if there was a shortage of steel but this wasn't ideal due to the fire risk if the bunker took a hit from incendiaries.

Once all this had been done, an outer mould was built around the reinforcements and the concrete poured in. This was done in a single, continuous operation that went on day and night, so as to create a bunker consisting of a single block of concrete without any seams or apparent weak points. Slave labour, armed with shovels, would help channel the concrete down chutes where it was then compacted with jack hammers. This meant that the whole process had to be carried out on site and traces of the

manufacturing process can still be seen on some beaches, where coastal erosion has exposed bunker foundations. The *Regelbau* concept formed the backbone of the Atlantic Wall. Freely translated, *Regelbau* means something down the line of 'Standard Build', and yet variation was truly the name of the game with close to 700 individual bunker types in the book at the end of the war, each with a specific task and identified by a unique number. This approach to fortifications allowed the contractor, Organisation Todt, quickly to adapt any stronghold or fortified area to meet local conditions (strategic, tactical and geographical) and to expand existing facilities without compromising their basic integrity.

By far the most common bunker types in Normandy were the tobruks. These were a family of small bunker designs so named after Italian fortifications used during the fighting around Tobruk in North Africa 1942. They were formally called ringstands, since they were based around a single circular or hexagonal opening reminiscent of a ring mount.

The tobruks were most commonly used as machine-gun pits for a single machine-gun team, but were also used as a firing pit for 50mm infantry mortars and some had searchlights mounted. While tobruks offered better protection to troops than open field entrenchments (the machine-guns usually had an armour-plated shield which protected the gunner around its 360 degree traverse), they obviously still were not as well protected as the fully enclosed machine-gun bunkers found in the *Festung* ports or on battery sites. Since their principal weapon was situated in a recess open to the elements, they could be disabled by a direct hit during an infantry attack, unlike the bunkers which could withstand everything except a close-quarter large calibre artillery strike.

There were two basic types of machine-gun *Tobrukstände*, the Vf58c and Vf58d, which differed slightly in construction details. The machine-gun *Tobrukstände* was often armed with an armour-shielded MG34 and also differed from the Vf61, which was designed for 50mm mortars and had a small concrete platform in the centre for supporting the mortar. Generally, tobruks offered a small shelter behind the ring opening to provide cover for the crew during attack, with a door in the side or rear of the structure which was usually reached by a couple of steps via the main bunker's exterior passage. Tobruks were only protected to Class Bl standards in terms of concrete thickness, ie 1.5m or less, so they were generally built flush to the ground so that the earth formed an additional layer of protection. In this situation, they presented a very difficult target for invading troops as they weren't easily visible at either ground level or from an elevated viewpoint.

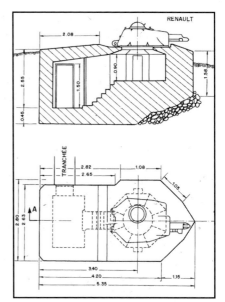

In some cases, tobruks were mounted along the seawall immediately along the water's edge. In these cases, the preferred solution was to construct thicker walls than the Class BI standards, though there were many cases where the lesser standards were followed for the sake of economy.

One version of the *Tobrukstände* commonly seen on the Normandy beaches was the *Panzerstellung*, equipped with a tank turret. These were usually based on the Vf67 but also included modified types, including a U-shaped style *Tobrukstände*. These were most commonly salvaged gun turrets from captured French tanks and the two most common types in Normandy were the World War I Renault FT tank turrets and the later APX-R turret.

The APX-R turret was developed by the Atelier de Puteaux in 1935 for the Renault firm, hence the APX-R designation. It was initially used on the Renault R-35 infantry tank and later fitted on the Hotchkiss H-35 and H-39 cavalry tank as well. It was also fitted with a

Turret from a French R-35 tank set on top of a *Tobrukstände* bunker.

PPLRX-180P armoured periscope in later models, which had a wider field of vision. The long-barrelled 37mm version wasn't common on the Atlantic Wall, however, being reserved largely for Renault and Hotchkiss tanks used by the *Heer* for fighting partisans in open countryside. While the two earlier types of turret with the short barrel were commonly used on the tobruks, these tank turrets also had a coaxial machine gun and, in some cases, the *Heer* would modify the turret by cutting open the observation dome at the top and installing a split hatch in its place. Few of these domes remain today, most having been claimed as scrap metal post war, but there are still a few examples dotted along the French coast.

The turret was manned by a single gunner but the leather strap seat that would be suspended below the gun originally was gradually phased out and the gunner eventually had to stand while on duty. The standard practice was to man these turrets with at least two soldiers, the second man assisting the gunner by feeding ammunition. There was no room to stow ammunition in most tobruks so it was usually kept in its actual shipping containers which, more often than not, were elongated wooden crates. To get access to the turret you could use a hatch built into the back though this, of course, would be highly dangerous during a battle so operators would normally retreat into the bunker itself if forced to leave in a hurry. Needless to say, if the bunker itself had been overrun, there was little prospect of escape.

As mentioned earlier, the strongpoints varied in layout to best exploit local terrain for increased protection. So, for example, the strongpoints on UTAH and OMAHA beaches were built in clusters behind the dunes across obvious paths leading off the beach in order to channel the Allied invaders into 'killing' zones. On SWORD and JUNO Beach in the British and Canadian sector, the defences were incorporated into seawalls and built into existing buildings which commonly ran all the way down to the edge of the beach or sea wall. The basic defensive concept for strongpoints was the so-called *Igel*, or hedgehog, philosophy with the bunkers, gun casemates and other positions arranged to provide interlocking fire.

Each position was assigned a sector of defence, and its weapons were also designed to cover the dead spaces of nearby positions. A typical strongpoint contained about five tobruks armed mainly with machine guns plus a few mortars, two to four gun positions, and two or three personnel, storage or command bunkers. Within a

Ringstände were usually incorporated onto the sides of casemates.

line of company strongpoints, there would usually be one or more of the heavy anti-tank gun bunkers for interlocking enfilade fire along the whole beach.

The most popular larger gun to be used in strongpoints was the 50 mm. Largely obsolete 50 mm tank guns, principally the KwK 39 and KwK40 which were originally fitted to the German *Panzerkampwagen* III medium tank, and the 50mm PaK38, an anti-tank gun used extensively on the Eastern front from 1941. The latter were remounted on pedestal mounts (*Sockellafetten*) for use in emplacements and fitted with a armour shield – these were primarily intended for use against landing craft.

The Pak38 were usually placed in Vf600 concrete emplacements for a 360 degree field of fire. These were octagonal concrete gun pits which were nominally more than four metres wide with recesses for ammunition in the front and side walls. The basic version had two access ways at the rear of the platform, but the modified Vf600 only had a single access way. In some cases, as at Crisbecq on the Cotentin Peninsula, target codes were painted on to the gun pit

A 50mm H667 casemate at OMAHA Beach designated E-1, one of the first to fall on D-Day. Here US Engineers use it as a command post.

walls so crews could bring their weapons to bear in rapid time having been directed by the observation bunkers.

Many of the H667 bunkers on the Atlantic Wall were positioned so they could provide enfilade fire along beaches rather than directly facing incoming forces. These bunkers required the excavation of about 150 cubic meters of soil and builders would have to pour around 380 cubic meters of concrete onto the 17 tonnes of steel rebar and 4.5 tonnes of other steel that made up the frame. Almost 150 of this type of bunker were constructed on the Atlantic Wall in early 1944, with more than a third in lower Normandy which was under the control of the Seventh Army. Those armed with the 88 mm PaK 43 or 41 were particularly lethal.

Construction of the H667 bunker was typical of the gun casemates found along the Normandy coast, basically a garage design with a large armoured access door in the rear and a large embrasure in the front to open a wide field of fire of around sixty degrees. The concrete walls were Category B, meaning they were two metres thick and were capable of resisting almost anything but a direct hit. That included most tank armament, though obviously a shell through the front embrasure would inevitably cause damage and inflict casualties as it ricocheted around the enclosed space. The armoured door to the rear could also be destroyed with accurate fire.

Most H677 bunkers had a concrete apron in front of the gun embrasure to prevent dirt being disturbed when the gun fired and

74

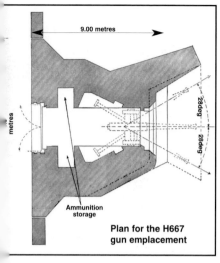

9.00 metres

metres

28deg

28deg

Ammunition storage

Plan for the H667 gun emplacement

thereby obscuring subsequent firing, but they were designed to be enclosed with earth on both sides, while at the rear of the bunker, further earthworks or a low protective concrete wall was erected to shield the rear armoured door. Generally, the roof was also covered with earth for camouflage purposes though the upper edge of the bunker had curved sections of steel rebar protruding that were used as hooks to attach camouflage nets. Generally, a camouflage net was extended over the entire front of the structure to hide the embrasure and protruding gun barrel. In some cases, the exposed concrete was also camouflage painted though its location would often define whether or not that was necessary.

This clearly shows the 50mm gun which poured enfilade fire across OMAHA Beach until it was knocked out. Prisoners are being used to clear up the damage.

50mm KwK 38 L/42 as seen above the beach at La Baule.

In common with the H677, the R501, R502 and R621 personnel bunkers were also built in abundance along the length of the Atlantic Wall in France, with over 1,000 constructed up to 1944.

The German R501 bunker was originally designed in 1939, as part of the planned Westwall defences against the French, the German response to the Maginot line. After construction of the Atlantic Wall was started in 1942, the R501 was built there as well, although it was later superseded by the type R621, which was roughly the same size but had more modern fittings. At least 1,519 type 501 bunkers were built during the Second World War.

All German bunkers tended to share features of the original *Festungspionier* design, such as the way the interior was laid out or the design of the ventilation system. As stated, the 500-series was originally developed for the Westwall but was easily adapted for use in the Atlantic Wall. The *Regelbau* (R) number designated the bunker's purpose. In the case of the R501 it was an *einfacher Gruppenunterstand*, which translates as a single squad dug-out in other words, a bunker in which one section of ten men could live.

One aspect of the R501 that could differ was the angle of the corners. Often, the sides were simply built into a square shape along with the curved roof edges where they joined. The advantage of this was that they were fairly simple to put together as no specialised joints were needed. But, by the time the bigger R502 was developed, a more complex, round finish was being used. Here, the whole corner of the bunker wall was rounded and roof corners were built into a spherical shape. The moulds for this were much more labour intensive but research had proved that the rounded corner was much stronger than the square and most bunkers had it incorporated by the end of 1943.

The R501 bunker was designed to house a single section of ten troops, while the R502 could house double that amount of personnel. As such, its main room was simple and rectangular, but the need to allow the bunker to be defended against both attackers and chemical weapons made necessary an elaborate entrance that took up a large amount of space. The R501 took up approximately ninety square metres of ground area, but only twenty square metres was for the use of the occupants, less than a quarter of the total area. The remainder of the site was taken up by the thick walls, entrance corridors, doorways and air locks.

The bunker primarily consisted of an entrance corridor, also known as the close-combat room, located in the rear wall, ie the wall that faced away from the most likely direction of enemy attack. This prevented enemy fire from landing directly in it, unintentionally or not. If possible, the entrance was protected by a 90 degree corner and overlooked by an embrasure. This opening, lined with wood to minimise the risk of ricochets, was usually protected by an armoured steel plate and could be used to inflict small arms fire. The corridor could be closed off by a metal bar door which prevented enemy troops from gaining access to the bunker but did not obstruct the firing ports set into the bunker wall. In later designs, gutters were fitted to the edge of the bunker entrance corridor, embrasures and air intakes which not only prevented rain water from collecting in doorways and on floors but also acted as a defence against flame throwers by diverting the inflammable fuel onto the walls.

One of the major differences between the 500-type bunkers and their successor, the 600-series, was that the entrance was on the same level of the bunker in the R501 and R502 but in the R621, the entrance was set much higher than the floor level, with steps leading down. This not only helped disguise the bunker itself but would also silhouette would-be assailants against the sky in normal circumstances. There was a decontamination chamber in case of chemical weapon attack, where soldiers could decontaminate themselves before entering the actual air lock – it otherwise led to a dead end. A locker with equipment to offset the effect of chemical weapons could be set up in this part of the bunker.

The air lock itself was a means to prevent gasses from chemical weapons from entering the bunker, by providing a place where the soldiers could be more thoroughly decontaminated before going into the main room. The air lock would also function as a defence against regular attacks, as it had a strong air-tight outer door made from three centimetre thick steel, with a rubber-sealed central firing port that also doubled as a viewing slot. This door was installed in

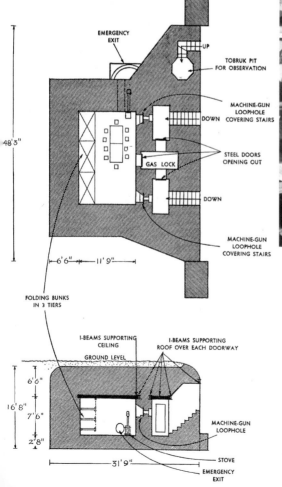

All the comforts of home and safe from bombs and shells.

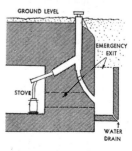

two halves, weighing almost 250 kilograms each, allowing the top and bottom to be opened separately (though a lip on the lower half meant it couldn't open any wider than the upper one). The logic behind this split opening was that any debris that might collected in the outside corridor might block the lower door but, unless it was a huge amount, the upper half could always be opened, allowing the bunker's occupants to escape. The air lock featured a purification filter and a pressure valve which increased the air pressure inside the air lock, forcing any gas through external intakes which were fitted with steel grills to prevent attackers using them as an access point for grenades.

The main barrack room was where the on-duty troops would spend what were normally twelve or fourteen hour shifts. Usually fitted out with bunk beds, a table and chairs, equipment lockers and a wood or coal-burning bunker stove for cooking and heating. Plus whatever personal touches the soldiers could smuggle in undetected. The stove had a

New arrivals entering a R621 shelter.

Ruhe und Besonnenheit...
und schnelle gründliche Entgiftung
erhalten dir Kampfkraft und Gesundheit!

Provisions were stockpiled in case of seige.

pipe which ran into the wall and connected to a chimney on the bunker roof. The chimney was angled at 90 degrees so that, if an assailant managed to drop a grenade inside, the device would be trapped and explode with minimal damage. The room also had a bunker ventilator mounted on the wall to provide fresh air and also to create over-pressure inside the bunker during a gas attack. This was a hand-cranked device that drew air into the bunker and, if required, through a filter.

The obligatory telephone to communicate with other bunkers inside the strongpoint or battery was next to the door in a protective wooden or metal casing alongside which was a voice pipe that usually led to the *Tobrukständetand*. A common warning above the phone read '*Achtung – Feind hört*

Opposite: Precautions against poisonous gas attack. A decontamination chamber carries the message:
Calm and Prudent Safety... Fast and thorough decontamination will maintain your combat readiness and health. **The room doubles as a store for arms and equipment. Note the flowers in the sink.**

81

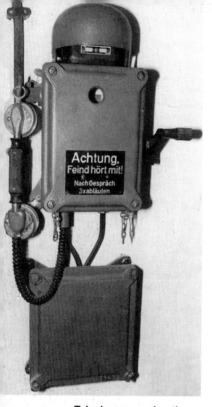

mit!' which roughly translates as 'Attention – the enemy is eavesdropping!' which was also the title of a popular German propaganda film released in 1940. In some crew rooms, a retractable periscope would allow soldiers to keep watch on their immediate surroundings without venturing outside and on rare occasions, wells were dug under the bunkers for fresh water though, more often than not, that had to be shipped in by tanker along with other supplies though some sites did have reinforced pits dug to form reservoirs. In the warmer climate of summer on the Atlantic Wall, these often doubled as swimming pools for the garrison. Toilet facilities were very basic for the rank and file, however. A covered bucket being the normal vessel of relief for all but those in command bunkers,

Telephone carrying the warning of the danger of the enemy listening in to any conversation.
Urinals, a part of the basic toilet facilities in some bunkers.

which had lavatories built into the design, though outside toilets or latrines were eventually installed in nearly all the strongpoints and batteries.

The main room was separated from the gas lock by another steel door, but much thinner than the outer door. It was in one piece, and consisted of thin steel plates riveted to a frame, instead of from a massive slab of steel. To create a gas-tight seal, a rubber gasket ran along the inside of the door frame while a small, glazed peep hole in the door itself gave a view into the gas lock.

To defend against attack, nearly all German bunkers had a firing port built into an interior wall, giving a field of fire straight down the entrance corridor. It consisted of a steel plate, 3 cm thick, set into a hole in the concrete of the wall. The plate had a firing hole measuring 30 cm x 22 cm in size and closed, from the inside, by a sliding shutter also made from 3 cm thick steel plate.

A *Kriegsmarine* officer using a periscope from inside a casemate.

In case the gas lock's outer door was completely blocked by debris, an escape tunnel was provided in the R501's right side wall. This was only 60 cm wide and 80 cm high and sealed by a steel door on the inside. It opened into a brick shaft of two metre diameter built onto the outer wall. Steel rungs on the bunker wall inside the shaft allowed the escaping soldiers to climb up onto the bunker's roof, though it's difficult to understand how designers imagined that would be any safer should the bunker be under attack. The shaft itself was normally filled with gravel, to prevent its use by the enemy with two brick walls inside the escape tunnel prevented the gravel from spilling into the bunker. When the tunnel was to be used, the soldiers would open the steel door, smash or pull down the brick walls, and let the gravel flood into the bunker.

Contrary to popular belief, most bunkers were not left in their unpainted, grey concrete colour during their use. The fact that they have this colour today is because the original paint has worn off due to sixty years' exposure to the weather. If the bunker was built in the open, a large part of it was covered by earth, to both blend it into the surrounding terrain and protect it from shellfire. The exposed concrete was then camouflaged with various coloured designs, the exact style depending on the surrounding area. The base colour was most likely dark yellow, as this colour can be seen on parts of surviving bunkers. Other colours used were darker with green and brown (similar to those used on vehicles) prominent. The yellow paint normally extended into the entrance corridor, in a triangle on the side walls from the top edge of the doorway down to the floor. The rest of the entrance corridor was painted like the interior.

Bunkers built in villages and towns, or near farms, were often disguised as civilian buildings. They received fake roofs and even chimneys made from wooden beams, planks and chicken wire, and had doors and windows painted onto their walls, often even with decorations such as curtains and flower vases visible inside. Although most of the fake roofs are quite apparent in contemporary photographs taken from ground level, they were very effective against aerial reconnaissance.

On the inside, bunkers were painted what would nowadays be known as egg shell white. Often, members of the garrison would decorate the walls with slogans or the badge of their regiment.

A command post and fire control centre painted to give the give the appearance of a local dwelling.

Grafitti is also common, much of it denouncing the Allies. The floor was often left as bare concrete, however, though some earlier bunkers did have brown asphalt tiles that acted as dampers to dull the effect of a nearby bomb blast. The internal walls would be lined with wood for the same reason with steel netting used in later constructions, including the gun casemates.

Interior metal fittings were almost always a dark green colour, while handles on cabinets, etc. were painted black. Stencilled signs in black inside the bunker indicated the purposes of the various rooms, as well as bunker identification numbers and warning signs. On many surviving bunkers, many of these are still clearly visible.

Construction of the R621 type, of which the R501 was the forerunner, began in January 1943 as the need to staff batteries and strongpoints around the clock against the threat of invasion became paramount. They typically required around 485 cubic metres of concrete, 23 tonnes of steel rebar and 3.7 tonnes of other steel. They were built with Standard B walls, ie two metres thick, and on flat ground if possible so that the entrance to any Tobruk, built on top of the structure, would be flush with the ground.

There were a number of modifications of this design, however, including the R62la with a pair of *Tobrukstände* gun positions at either end of the bunker. The R62I was part of a family of similar personnel shelters, the related R622 *Doppelgruppenstand* (double section/group/squad position) being nearly identical in appearance except that it was large enough for two adjacent rooms to accommodate two groups of men, twenty in total. The R62I can be distinguished from the R622 in that it usually had four circular ventilation covers between the two entry ways while the R622 had six. These two types of bunkers made up nearly a third of all fortifications built for the army along the Atlantic Wall.

KRIEGSMARINE

The initial role of the *Kriegsmarine* coastal artillery was to decimate the invasion force before it reached the shoreline. The navy had traditionally viewed shore-based defences as an extension of the fleet and so deployed the batteries along the coast where they could most easily engage attacking surface vessels. The gun casemates were connected by electric cable to an elaborate fire-control/observation post which possessed optical rangefinders and aiming systems that could plot trajectories against moving targets. Their presence did not comfort all interested parties, however. The *Heer* viewed the naval batteries as the battleships of the dunes and argued that their placement so close to the shore made them immediately visible to enemy warships, and therefore in range of naval gunfire. In addition, the proximity to the shore also made the guns vulnerable to airborne or infantry attack in the event of an amphibious assault or concerted invasion.

The army's attitude to coastal batteries was based on the premise that they were located primarily to repulse an amphibious attack and not engage in a protracted exchange with heavy armour based at sea. As a result, the army tended to concentrate their batteries further inland unless there was a strategic need to arrange covering fire for particular sectors of the coast.

An example of this was at Pointe du Hoc, an elevated promontory protected by cliffs with a clear line of sight to neighbouring beaches. The army's control bunkers were commonly less complex than the naval bunkers. They did house rangefinders and targeting devices but could not engage with moving targets as easily as the naval batteries. The *Heer* big guns also placed more emphasis on radio connections with other army units, relying on artillery forward observers to assist in the direction of fire against targets that weren't visible to the gunners themselves.

It was not just in tactics that the Germany army and navy disagreed. The two branches of the armed forces had very different views on the technical aspects of coastal large calibre guns. The navy preferred an enclosed gun that could survive a prolonged engagement with naval forces and they even employed warship turrets, salvaged from damaged ships or spares, in locations where the bedrock was sufficient to support the weight. For example, the *Kriegsmarine* used a 380 mm gun turret from the French First World War Courbet class battleship *Jean-Bart* in a battery near Le Havre.

Of course, it was impossible to build new turrets on the Atlantic Wall with the majority of the manufactured armour plate being used on tanks and ships and this was to lead to the development of casemates as an alternative to protect the guns and their crews against everything but the most accurate shelling and bombing.

During 1943, naval engineers began to experiment with a new mix of reinforced concrete using wire under stress instead of the usual steel bars. This promised to be significantly more flexible, sparking hopes that a fully traversable concrete turret could be

Kriegsmarine fire control centre laid out to resemble the operational areas of a battleship.

developed. The limitations of traverse in casemates, which generally only offered a narrow firing window, was a major stumbling block and severely hampered a gun's manoeuvrability. It also offered a distinct target to mortars and the petards of the AVRE tanks. But, though some experimental turrets were built behind the front lines in early 1944 and one near Fort Vert, Calais in April of that year, the innovation came too late to influence the war.

The army did not favour fixed guns like the navy and preferred to use conventional field artillery. This was based on the premise that the batteries could be easily moved from non-threatened areas to reinforce the defences in sectors under attack. The army was basing its tactics on previous British amphibious assaults (there was no example of an American assault to study), such as at Gallipoli in the First World War, where the seaborne invasion developed into a protracted military campaign.

At first, the *Heer* used *Kessel* mounts based on the First World War gun pits, which were simply circular concrete-lined holes in the ground with recesses for charges and ammunition. The gun itself was completely exposed, but the gun pit was surrounded by protected crew shelters, ammunition bunkers and a fire-control bunker.

As Allied air activity over the French coast increased in intensity, the vulnerability of these batteries to air attack became the subject of some concern. At face value, it appeared that the navy's reinforced casemates offered better protection from air attack than the open kettle gun pits. But, the testimony of gun crews suggested this wasn't necessarily the case and structural engineers backed up their claims that the casemates could concentrate the blast of any bomb or large shell that landed near the opening, proving deadly to those inside, while the guns in open pits were comparatively safe during an air raid except for the rare occasions when the gun and

Gun crew running running out an obsolete captured French 25mm anti-tank gun of 1940 vintage.

its crew took a direct hit. Following the Dieppe raid, however, the policy shifted to encase all army batteries in casemates. These resembled the navy casemates in almost all aspects except that they were generally built with a large garage-type door at the rear to allow removal of the gun inside for transfer to other sites in the sector if needed.

There were several classifications of concrete thickness used in German bunkers, most of which had been drawn up by army fortification engineers during the construction of the Westwall *programm*. The highest level for tactical fortifications was class A, which used steel-reinforced concrete to a thickness of 3.5 metres. This was costly and time-consuming to produce so tended to be confined to large, high-priority structures such as the U-boat pens at St Nazaire and heavy gun batteries in the Pas-de-Calais. The latter category included *Batterie Todt* and *Batterie Lindemann*. But most fortifications which faced the Atlantic were built to the B standard, which meant walls were two metres thick. That, in theory, gave the bunkers protection from artillery shells up to 210 mm and bombs up to 500 kg in weight.

Many minor bunkers, which often included those regarded as non-essential (crew shelters, stores, etc.) were built to the slightly less impressive Bl standard, though these were often at least partially buried to provide additional protection. As the war progressed and steel became more difficult to acquire, engineers would try to cut back on the amount needed and it wasn't uncommon for internal doors to be made of wood.

The basic construction method remained the same for the casemates as well as the bunkers, only on a grander scale. The type R685 casemate, for example, which was designed to house either a 210 mm or a 128 mm anti-aircraft gun, would still be built by the concrete being poured over steel rebars between planks or beams of wood arranged into its respective different quarters and levels.

The type R685 consisted of a gun room with recesses for ammunition. Its walls were built to class A specification (3.5 metres thick), as was the roof – both were then covered with earth to a depth of, if possible, at least 60 cm. The embrasure, underneath the familiar stepped roof, allowed a traverse of sixty degrees and an elevation of forty-five degrees. A number of similar casemates had embrasures for a traverse of 90 degrees or even 120 degrees when it was realised that a restrictive angle of fire would make the casemate vulnerable to attack from the sides or rear but, on and after D-Day, these modifications proved largely in vain.

Most casemates, even those housing the massive guns in the Pas de Calais, were built using the same construction techniques, but the giants turms in the batteries of the Pas de Calais were also built on several levels which meant incorporating both bunker and casemate design.

For example, the four casemates at *Batterie Todt* (formerly *Siegfried*), which housed 380 mm Skoda C34 turreted guns, had foundations which began with the digging of exterior drains and interior ventilation shafts. Wooden boards or shutters were then put in place to form the outer shell of the ground floor which contained the diesel generator, billet rooms for eighteen men an armoury, a canteen, workshops and a store for fuel. Ventilation shafts also played a vital role in a casemate as air inside the emplacement would be sucked out when the gun fired and had to be replenished. A lift shaft and stairwell connected the lower level to the ammunition room which contained the shells for the gun and an offset room for the charge cartridges. Before the concrete was poured, an overhead pulley system was anchored into the rebars that was to form the ceiling of the shell room to allow for easier transportation of the armaments to the exterior railway track. This track, thought to be initially used to move concrete mixers into position above the site for pouring, ran inside the main casemate to the edge of the turntable on which sat the gun itself. The whole revolved around a giant driveshaft.

The gun and its armoured turret were anchored to a steel chassis on the turntable, pivoting for firing on greased bearings on either side of the barrel. Both the chassis and barrel had to be transported from their place of manufacture and lifted into place via cranes attached to tall gantries which were rolled into position above the casemates. They had to be fitted and tested before the armour-plated embrasure cap could be bolted into place and the concrete poured which would form the ceiling and roof.

Camouflage could then be applied, in the case of *Batterie Todt* that included the painting of houses and trees on the casemates as well as netting which was hung from the protruding end of the existing steel rebars. The disguise was surprisingly effective, especially from distance or from the air. Impressive in sight as these concrete monsters were, however, they were to prove just as vulnerable as the rest of the fortifications on the Atlantic Wall.

Chapter Five

THE FOUNDING OF HOBART'S 'FUNNIES'

P ERCY CLEGHORN STANLEY HOBART was born in the
Kumaon hill station of Naini Tal on 14 June 1885, where
his father was a key figure in the Indian Civil Service. His
birth was to set a trend for great military leaders to emanate
from this remote outpost of the British
Empire.

Just two years later, 1887, General
The Lord Ismay, Winston Churchill's
chief military advisor and subsequently
the first Secretary General of NATO,
also began his life in Naini Tal; in 1903
Orde Charles Wingate, famous for his
creation of the Chindits and undercover
operations against the Japanese in
south-east Asia during the Second
World War, was also born and spent his
early life among the Himalayan
foothills.

After an education served at Clifton
College Boarding School in Bristol,
which in the late nineteenth century
specialised in science, mathematics and
engineering, Hobart followed in the
footsteps of British Army Commander-
in-Chief Douglas Haig by enrolling at
the Royal Military Academy in
Woolwich and was commissioned into
the Royal Engineers in 1904. In 1906 he
was posted to India where he joined the
Bengal Sappers and Miners.

**Major-General Sir Percy
Cleghorn Stanley Hobart KBE
CB DSO MC**

In January 1915 he went to France with the 1st Indian
Expeditionary Force and won the MC at Neuve Chapelle, later
being transferred to Mesopotamia in January 1916, where he was
awarded the DSO.

Hobart was a forward thinker with a strong personality and on more than one occasion these characteristics led him into trouble with his superiors, many of whom failed to appreciate that changes he was advocating was inevitable and that future wars were unlikely to be fought on the same lines as in 1914-1918.

Hobart – 'Hobo' to his military colleagues – returned to India in 1921 and, convinced by the belief that any future wars would be won by the tank, transferred to the Royal Tank Corps on its formation in 1923. After four years as an instructor at the Staff College in Quetta, he returned to England, initially as second in command of the 4th Battalion of the Tank Corps and later as CO of the 2nd Battalion. In 1934 he raised and commanded the 1st Tank Brigade and in four years, evolved new tactical methods based on mobility and speed, linked to new techniques for command and control.

After a short spell at the War Office, 'Hobo' was appointed Director of Military Training and in 1938 was sent to Egypt to raise what was to become the 7th Armoured Division. But his advanced views on the use of armour did not find favour in all quarters and in 1939 he was 'retired' by chief critic Sir Archibald Wavell, at the age of fifty-four. Of course, the effectiveness of his methods and training were to be well illustrated by his protégés in subsequent years.

However, his active military career was far from over and in 1941, after a short period as a corporal in the ranks of the Home Guard, he was recalled at the specific order of Winston Churchill and offered command of the 11th Armoured Division. Churchill had been influenced by the representations made by Hobart's mentor, the highly-acclaimed military analyst Captain Sir Basil H. Liddell Hart, who then had to persuade a disillusioned Hobart to come out of 'retirement' and accept the post. After the ill-fated raid on Dieppe in 1942, the need for specialist armoured equipment became ever more obvious and, in April 1943, Hobart was given the task of raising, organising and training the 79th Armoured Division for the invasion of Europe in 1944.

At the outbreak of war in 1939, the Royal Engineers had no armoured vehicles but it quickly became clear that change was needed. As a first step, armoured scout cars were issued to field squadrons of armoured divisions and these were followed by armoured personnel carriers. But it was accepted that some form of engineer tank was required to enable Royal Engineers personnel to force routes through minefields and over or through defended anti-tank obstacles.

At the outbreak of war, tanks were not available for experimental work but as a compromise for a particular operation, some were 'lent' to the Sappers so they could advance developments, though that was under the condition the tanks were returned to base in their original condition. Consequently fittings which could be mounted and removed in a matter of hours were the order of the day.

79TH ARMOURED DIVISION

The formation of the 79th Armoured Division, under Hobart, with massive emphasis on a tank development programme was long overdue. With a brief to 'co-ordinate the development of armoured assault techniques and equipment', 'Hobart's Funnies' were born.

The development of the Armoured Vehicle Royal Engineers (AVREs) has been attributed to an original idea put forward by Lieutenant J. J. Denovan of the Royal Canadian Engineers, but attached to the Special Devices Branch of the Department of Tank Design. His plan was for a tank with as much of the standard internal equipment stripped, leaving storage space for the sapper's equipment, tools and explosives. The Churchill was chosen because of its combination of

The Churchill was chosen because of its combination of a large interior, thick armour and a side access door. The example depicted, MkVII, was not converted to AVRE specifications at the time of the Normandy inlandings.

a large interior, thick armour and a side access door, and a prototype was developed for the Department of Tank Design by the 1st Canadian Mechanical Engineer Company.

A demonstration on Hankley Common at Farnham in Surrey on 25 February, 1943 showed what the engineers had in mind. A Churchill tank with the internal ammunition storage removed and a new side door that unfolded to become an armoured screen was driven up to a concrete wall. The sappers emerged from the tank, placed and lit General Wade explosive charges on the wall, and then retreated, still undercover, into the tank. The resulting hole was large enough to drive the tank through.

The 290 mm muzzle loading mortar, the 'petard' with which the Churchill AVRE were to become synonymous, was developed separately by Colonel Blacker, the designer of the Blacker Bombard, a spigot mortar built for the Home Guard. He was asked to design a version of the mortar that could be mounted on a tank, and produced a weapon that could fire a 40 lb high explosive shell squash head (HESH) known as the Flying Dustbin. A massive spring in the turret soaked up the twenty tons of recoil and used the energy to reset the mortar. At the Hankley Common demonstration, the mortar was mounted on a Churchill tank and, after using shells fused for air burst to clear a twenty-eight feet wide gap through a minefield, the mortar then fired twelve shells directly at a six feet thick concrete wall, again creating a gap wide enough for a tank.

The two designs were merged to create the AVRE. Around 700 were produced by converting Churchill Mk IIIs and IVs, of which 180 had been completed by the time of the Normandy landings, where they were used by the 1st Assault Brigade of the 79th Armoured Division. The AVRE was given standard attachment points that could be used to carry a wide range of specialised equipment, including fascine carriers that could drop their brushwood bundles into ditches or at the base of barriers, a variety of mine sweeping devices, a Small Box Girder bridge, 'Bobbin' carpet laying tanks and the 'Goat' explosive device.

The AVRE played an important part in the success of the British and Canadian landings on D-Day, where their spigot mortar was especially valuable, destroying a number of German strong points including guns based at the sanatorium at Le Hamel which were targeting the Hampshire and Dorset regiments coming ashore on Gold Beach. They continued to operate successfully during the

A Petard and projectile nicknamed the 'Flying Dustbin' HESH round.

Churchill AVRE carrying a fascine for overcoming anti-tank ditches.

campaign in north-western Europe, and later versions of the AVRE tank remained in use long after the Churchill had been retired.

By the end of October 1943, various engineer units had been renamed and transferred into this division as 1st Assault Brigade Royal Engineers. This brigade comprised three Assault Regiments, each with four Assault Squadrons, plus an Assault Park Squadron. The structure was to remain undisturbed up to the Normandy landings in June 1944.

The formation of the Funnies started with the need to create a series of modern siege engines to lead the assault on the beach defences of the French coast. A rapid sweeping away of the obstacles and defenders in the British sectors was deemed crucial as the Normandy terrain lent itself to a rapid counter-attack by German armour.

Field Marshal Sir Alan Brooke made the decision in 1943 to create these new units and responsibility for the conversion of vehicles and the training of crews to use them was given to armoured warfare expert Percy Hobart. It's a misunderstanding to presume all of the Funnies' equipment was a product of the Royal Engineers' imagination, however. Many of the ideas had already been tried, tested or were in experimental development both by

Sherman Crab Flail tank and Churchill box girder bridge adaptation.

Britain and other nations. For example, the Scorpion flail tank (a modified Matilda tank) had already been used during the North African campaign to clear paths through German minefields. However, it was far less reliable than the Sherman Crab. Some of the Soviet Union's T-34 tanks had been modified with mine-rollers. Close-support tanks, bridge-layers and fascine carriers had also been developed elsewhere. However, the Funnies easily possessed the most comprehensive and wide-ranging assortment of engineering oddities.

By early 1944, Hobart could demonstrate to Eisenhower and Montgomery (Hobart's brother-in-law) a brigade each of swimming Duplex Drive tanks (**DD**), **Crab** mine clearers, and AVRE (Engineer) tanks along with a regiment of **Crocodile** flame-throwing tanks.

Montgomery considered that the US forces should use them, and offered them a half-share of all the vehicles available, but the take-up was minimal. Eisenhower was in favour of the amphibious tanks but passed on the decision to take up option on the others to General Bradley, who delegated it to his staff officers. In the end, US forces didn't order any of the adapted armour because it was thought that their operation would require specialised training and a support regiment, though there were also rumours at the time that Bradley didn't believe they'd be effective under battleground conditions.

The designs incorporated by the British were all used on modified forms of the Churchill or the Sherman tank. By 1943, both were available in large numbers. The Churchill offered a solid, if unspectacular, cross-country performance, heavy armour and a roomy interior for its crew, while the American Sherman was renowned for its mechanical reliability. Among the many specialist vehicles and their attachments, the most well-known were: The AVRE, or Armoured Vehicle, Royal Engineers. This was a Churchill tank adapted to attack German defensive fortifications and, therefore, pivotal in the destruction of the Atlantic Wall. The crew included two Royal Engineers who could easily leave and enter the tank through its armoured side hatches, which provided cover while they laid charges. As described earlier, the AVRE had its main gun replaced by a Petard Spigot Mortar which could fire a forty pound (18 kg) high explosive-filled projectile 150 yards (137 metres). The 'Dustbin' was specifically designed to destroy concrete obstacles such as roadblocks and bunkers and proved highly successful in the wake of D-Day, but it did have its drawbacks. For example, the weapon had to be reloaded externally, by opening a hatch and sliding a round into the mortar tube from the hull and the Petard's relative short-range meant that crews were vulnerable if the defences had armour-piercing weaponry at their disposal or employed snipers.

The AVREs' role was not solely as attack weapons, however. They were also used to carry and operate equipment such as the **Bobbin**, a reel of 10-foot (3m) wide canvas cloth reinforced with steel poles carried in front of the tank and able to be unrolled across the ground to form a path, so that following vehicles (and the AVRE itself) would not sink into the soft ground of the beaches during an amphibious landing.

Then there was the fascine, a bundle of wooden poles or rough brushwood lashed together with wires and carried in front of the tank that could be released to fill a ditch or form a step. Metal pipes in the centre of the fascine allowed drainage so that the temporary plug would not become waterlogged.

The AVRE could also carry a small box girder that became an instant assault bridge. Also held in place in front of the tank, the box girder could be dropped to span a gap of up to thirty feet (9.1 metres) in thirty seconds ensuring an invasion force would not lose momentum due to uneven terrain.

The **Bullshorn** plough excavated the ground in front of the tank, exposing and rendering harmless land mines, while a further

There were several modifications tried to overcome the damage caused by land mines the tank was finding and exploding.

Crews from two AVREs placing explosives (known as General Wade charges) against a concrete barrier.

Following the explosion a Churchill tank demonstrates the ease at which a nine foot high concrete barrier can be overcome.

adaptation was known as the **Double Onion**. This comprised two large demolition charges on a metal frame that could be placed against a concrete wall and detonated once the AVRE had retired a safe distance. Why the unusual nickname? Typical army humour, its single charge predecessor was known as 'the Carrot'.

The **Crocodile** was a Churchill tank modified by the fitting of a flame-thrower in place of the standard turret machine gun. An armoured trailer, towed behind the tank, carried 400 gallons (1,800 litres) of fuel. The flame-thrower had a range of over 120 yards (110 metres) and was largely used to clear bunkers and buildings where opposition troops were holed up.

The **ARK** was a rough abbreviation of Armoured Ramp Carrier. This, again, was a Churchill but unrecognisable as such, the turret having been removed so that extendable ramps could be fitted on each side of the tank; following vehicles could then drive up the ramps and over the ARK to scale obstacles or embankments.

Moving on to the Sherman tanks, there was the Crab which was equipped with a mine flail, a rapidly-rotating cylinder of weighted chains that exploded mines in the path of the tank. Each exploding mine would destroy one of the flail chains, so it was statistically inevitable that sooner or later the Crab would be disabled by a mine missed by the flails. The DD tank, short for Duplex Drive, which had a transmission that could be adapted for use on water as well as land and was able to 'swim' after being launched from a landing craft several miles from the beach.

The flamethrowing tank named the Crocodile was one of the early adaptations of the Churchill tank.

Duplex Drive DD

Hungarian Nicholas Straussler was the engineer credited with the development of the DD tank used by Allied forces during the Second World War. Between 1928 and 1933, Straussler headed a company called Folding Boats and Structures Ltd, patenting a number of flotation devices. He became a British citizen in 1933 and throughout the 1930s worked with Alvis Cars and armoured vehicle manufacturers Vickers-Armstrong as well as various Hungarian companies. His work for Alvis also involved designing armoured cars such as the Alvis Straussler AC2 and the Alvis Straussler AC3 as well as bomb trolleys for the RAF. His most important work was for Vickers-Armstrong, which included the design of accessories for tanks. The engineering solutions he produced tended to be innovative, though sometimes

Nicholas Straussler.

arguably lacking in practicability. He adapted his flotation device to develop collapsible floats that could be used to either construct a pontoon bridge or make a light tank amphibious. Trials conducted by the War Office showed that an adapted tank, propelled by an outboard motor, 'swam' to some degree

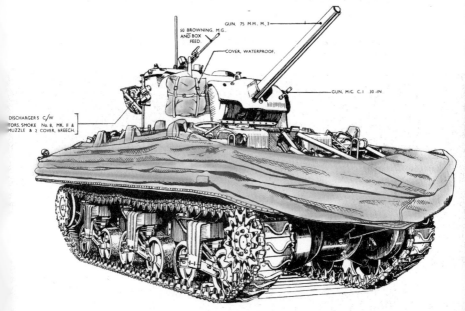

A Sherman DD with semi-inflated swimming skirt.

but the floats needed to float a tank were almost the same size as the tank itself and would never have been practical to transport in an amphibious assault. Indeed, such floats made a tank too wide to launch itself into the sea from an off-shore landing craft. Undeterred, Straussler devised an alternative, the flotation screen. This was a folding canvas screen, supported by metal hoops with rubber tubes filled with compressed air providing the buoyancy. The screen covered the top half of the tank and, when collapsed, was designed to leave the tank's mobility and combat effectiveness unimpaired.

Straussler was given a Tetrarch tank for trials and it was fitted with a screen together with a marine propeller that took its drive from the tank's engine. The two forms of propulsion – propeller and tracks – gave rise to the term Duplex Drive or DD.

The first trial of the DD Tetrarch took place in June 1941 in Hendon Reservoir in North London, with General Alan Brooke attending on behalf of the Army. Sea trials of the Valentine tank, near Hayling Island in Hampshire, followed and the go-ahead was given to develop a production DD tank based on the Vickers-Armstrong Valentine tank. This version never saw combat, however, being used to train crews who subsequently served in the DD versions of the Mark 4 Sherman, one of a number of modified, special purpose tanks used by Hobart's Funnies that saw action during and after D-Day.

Straussler continued to work on adapting the DD system to other British vehicles, including the Churchill, the Cromwell and the Centurion but none of these went into production and post-war tanks were generally too heavy to be made amphibious with a flotation screen.

After the war, he oversaw a variety of projects although many were still connected in some way with amphibious vehicles. They included the Lypsoid Tyre, a very low-pressure, run-flat tyre that saw some use with military and construction vehicles. He continued working into his old age, filing the last of his thirty patents in 1964, just two years before his death.

Other tank derivations included the BARV (Beach Armoured Recovery Vehicle) which was adapted from a Sherman M4A2 tank which had been waterproofed and had the turret replaced by a tall armoured superstructure. Able to operate in 9 feet (2.7 metres) of deep water, the BARV was designed to remove vehicles that had become broken-down or swamped in the surf and were blocking access to the beaches. They were also used to re-float small landing craft that had 'beached' in low water. Strictly speaking, BARV's were not 'Funnies' in the strictest sense of the meaning as they were developed and operated by the Royal Electrical and Mechanical Engineers and not the 79th Armoured Division but they are included in this chapter for ease of summation.

A Beach Armoured Recovery vehicle.

The 79th Armoured Division also operated the British version of the American LVT4 which was an armoured amphibious landing vehicle and armoured bulldozer, a conventional caterpillar bulldozer fitted with armour to protect the driver and engine. The bulldozer's main function was to clear the invasion beaches of obstacles and to make roads accessible by clearing rubble and filling in bomb craters. All the conversions were carried out by a Caterpillar importer, Jack Olding & Company Ltd of Hatfield.

Olding, a veteran of the First World War, was a huge supporter of the British war effort. A former dealer in luxury cars, he adapted his Hertfordshire factory to produce a variety of bespoke military heavy plant machinery including graders and scrapers which were used to build roads, bases and fortifications as well as creating a channel so that large sections of Mulberry harbour could be floated across to France to aid the invasion.

Olding also sponsored a school to train military personnel in the use of Caterpillar equipment and this developed into the RAF Airfield Construction training establishment at what was to become RAF Mill Green. The armoured bulldozer's contribution to the Allied war effort can not be overemphasised, with even Dwight D Eisenhower in his book *Crusade in Europe* pointing out, 'Four other pieces of equipment that most senior officers came to regard as among the most vital to our success in Africa and Europe were the bulldozer, the jeep, the 2.5 ton truck, and the C-47 airplane. Curiously, none of these is designed for combat.'

The Centaur Bulldozer was an obsolete Centaur tank with the turret removed and fitted with a winch-operated bulldozer blade. Again these were produced because of a need for an obstacle-clearing vehicle but, unlike a conventional bulldozer, was also fast enough to keep up with tank formations and had enough armour

Centaur Bulldozer.

to withstand sustained combat conditions. However, they hadn't been fully developed by D-Day and weren't issued to the 79th Armoured Division until the latter part of 1944, where they were used in the liberation of Belgium.

Another piece of heavy equipment that came into operation in the latter months of the war was the Canal Defence Light. This was a powerful carbon-arc searchlight carried on several types of tank

inside a modified turret. The name of the device was a deliberate misnomer, however, as its true purpose was to blind defenders during a night attack. The light was concentrated through a small slit in the armour, meaning the chance of damage

Commander-in-Chief Sir Bernard Montgomery with Brigadier Duncan, commander of 30th Armoured Brigade with Major General Hobart.

by enemy fire was minimal. It was to come into its own in support of the Sherwood Yeoman Rangers and US 333rd Infantry Division during the attack on Geilenkirchen in November 1944.

Much of the 79th Armoured Division landed in Normandy, more of which later, early on the morning of 6 June 1944 as a special assault team in support of the three infantry divisions on the British/Canadian sector. This assault support role, under the continuing command of Hobart, was maintained until the end of the war.

By May 1945, the 79th Armoured Division found itself in the Hamburg area. By August, the division was being disbanded though did enjoy a brief re-incarnation in Suffolk as the Specialised Armour Development Establishment (SADE), with Hobart at the helm.

There was, of course, a new enemy at the door in the shape of the Soviet Bloc but the role of armour in any new conflict had changed and March 1946 saw Percy Hobart put out to grass again for the second time at the age of sixty.

'Hobo' still wasn't ready for retirement, however, and with brother-in-law Field Marshal Montgomery as the new Chief of the Imperial General Staff, Hobart was appointed Lieutenant Governor of the Royal Hospital in Chelsea. In 1947 he was appointed a Colonel Commandant of The Royal Armoured Corps. He left Chelsea in 1953 but two years later fell seriously ill.

It was to prove one battle too many for the old warhorse, whom US 9th Army commander General William H. Simpson described as; 'The outstanding British officer of high rank that I met during the war.' Percy Hobart died 19 February 1957, aged seventy-one.

Monty did not always see eye-to-eye with Hobart but he was fulsome in his praise of 'Hobo' in his obituary in the *Times* and Liddell Hart also paid tribute to Major General Sir Percy Hobart KBE, CB, DSO, MC on his death:

He was one of the few soldiers I have known who could be rightly termed a military genius.

Chapter Six

FROM LE HAVRE TO DUNKERQUE

THE MARCH NORTH and the taking of the fortified ports between Normandy and the Pas de Calais was to claim many more Allied and German lives but the dam had been broken and the trickle of troops into Normandy had become a flood as Cherbourg and Caen finally fell and the British Mulberry Harbour at Arromanches allowed reserve forces to support the initial assault troops.

Le Havre and its promontory had already proved a thorn in the side of the invasion forces. Shells had been aimed at the landing beaches from within its walls and E-boats and U-boats had continued operating out of its harbour, threatening Allied shipping bringing supplies across the Channel.

Right: A 138 mm gun of former French battery Dollemard at Le Harve manned by Germans defending the port in 1944.

Below: Overlooking Le Havre. This observation bunker has three floor levels with range finding equipment trained on the Channel.

Boulevard Clémenceau, Le Havre.

LE HAVRE

British I Corps was charged with the capture of Le Havre with the assault the responsibility of the 49th and 51st Divisions, each with a generous allotment of assault troops. Brigadier Duncan with Headquarters 30th Armoured Brigade commanded all units of the 79th Armoured Division involved in the operation.

HMS *Warspite* supporting the capture of the Atlantic Wall strongpoints.

The port had a garrison of 12,000 plus and was surrounded by strong fortifications, including an anti-tank ditch, a deep minefield on either side of the ditch, and multiple strongpoints. At a quarter to six in the evening of 10 September, 1944, Operation ASTONIA was launched to liberate Le Havre. HMS *Warspite* and HMS *Erebus* engaged coastal batteries defending the port and RAF bombers dropped 5,000 tons of bombs prior to

Waiting for the order to advance these officers observe the bombardment of the defences by sea and air.

the infantry launching their assault. The bombing of Le Havre was a shameful episode that did General Crocker no credit. The German garrison commander had offered to allow all civilians to be evacuated, but the British refused to let them out. Over 3,000 French civilians were killed by the RAF, both the town and the very harbour installations apparently so badly needed by the allies were wrecked and not one German soldier was killed.

The attack was divided into two phases: firstly to penetrate the

Churchill tanks of 7 Royal Tank Regiment in position ready for the advance on Le Havre.

Armour moving up to the Forming Up Point including a Churchill AVRE in the foreground.

Below: Assault team of Seaforth Highlanders, 51st Highland Division, forming up for an attack on the right flank of the assault on Le Havre. Behind them is a Sherman Crab and an AVRE.

Sherman Crabs of A Squadron 22 Dragoons moving up to join the AVREs at the F.U.P. (Forming Up Point) .

Crocodiles of A Squadron, 141 Royal Armoured Corps, going through gap code named 'Laura'. The assault team about to attack German Strongpoint 5 below the wood.

German defences to allow further forces to widen the front and, secondly, to cement gains and capture the city. With the assistance of specialist units from the 79th Armoured Division and the 1st Canadian Armoured Carrier Regiment, such as Kangaroos and Sherman Crabs, the first part of the assault went largely without a

Three lanes swept of mines were numbered 1 to 3 and they went by the code name LAURA. Here Churchills of 7 Royal Tank Regiment moving to attack along the lanes.

GERMAN ROAD BLOCK 5

Lane 3   Lane 2   Lane 1

The height of the action with Crocodiles subduing the German defensive positions for the attacking infantry.

A Petard-armed Churchill blasts a German concrete bunker to destruction. Photograph taken from another Churchill during the battle.

Men of 7th Royal Tank Regiment watch as RAF Lancaster bombers of 617 Squadron begin their bombing run over the ring of defences around Le Havre.

hitch with the flails creating gaps through the minefield and anti-tank ditches bridged.

The 49th West Riding Infantry Division breached the north-eastern section of the Le Havre perimeter first, swiftly followed by the 51st Highland Infantry Division attacking from the north. The assault was costly for the specialised armour, however, with the

Men of I Lothians aboard a flail tankSherman Crab II return to rally area.

79th Armoured Division losing thirty-four Crab anti-mine flail tanks, two command tanks and six AVRE vehicles.

The first phase continued into a second day with further bombing raids and armour engaging the last strongpoints of the outer defences. These finally surrendered at two o'clock in the

German officers arrive to surrender in an Stuart light tank.

Prisoners of war at Le Havre.

afternoon after they were threatened with the use of Churchill Crocodile flame-throwing tanks. On the third day of the assault, the town centre was finally cleared and the German garrison commander surrendered with remarkably few military casualties. However, the cost to the civilian population had been more drastic and Le Havre had been pretty much levelled and was therefore almost useless as a port of supply and disembarkation for years to come. Operation ASTONIA did serve as an example, however, that the Allies were not prepared to wait out German surrender in France and other ports were to suffer a similar fate in the following months.

Major General Barker commanding 49th Infantry Division after receiving the German surrender.

Damaged port installations at Boulogne

BOULOGNE

Boulogne was another of the Channel ports to be designated as a *Festunghäfe* (fortress port) by Adolf Hitler. The idea was that these would be heavily fortified towns manned by troops committed to fight to the end, thus denying the Allies the use of the facilities and committing opposition troops to a containment role. In practice, Boulogne's landward defences were incomplete, many of its garrisons were second-rate and demoralised by their isolation and the obvious inability of the *Heer* to rescue or support them in any meaningful way. In the event, none of the defenders fought to the end, preferring to surrender when confronted by overwhelming forces.

The city and port of Boulogne is sited at the mouth of the River Liane, which flows north into the sea. The Liane splits the city in two, with the western side forming a high peninsular between the river and the coast. High ground surrounds the city and most of it had been fortified over the centuries. The most significant artillery batteries in the Second World War were at La Tresorerie, Mont Lambert and Herquelingue with various fortifications on the coastal peninsular.

Ferdinand Heim had been appointed as commander of Boulogne only a few weeks before the port became isolated by the Allies' advance through northern France. The city's fixed defences were formidable but little had been done on the landward side apart from some hastily-built field defences and they were to be cruelly exposed by Operation WELLHIT.

In the days preceding the attack on Boulogne, attempts were made by air and artillery bombardment to weaken the German defences. In the final moments before the Canadian infantry advanced, several hundred heavy and medium bombers from the

Leutnantgeneral Ferdinand Heim.

RAF and USAF instigated a creeping barrage to clear a path into the city but this proved relatively ineffective. On his capture, Heim said that 'amongst personnel, casualties were almost negligible'.

Defences had suffered little damage and, in addition, bomb craters were impeding armoured vehicles supporting the infantry attacks and it was to take a week to eventually subdue all resistance. The Canadian plan of attack intended that the northern and southern defences of Boulogne be occupied while the main force pushed into the city from the east.

Since German artillery at La Tresorerie posed a threat to the main assault, an attack by the North Shore Regiment on the battery would precede the main attack. Two infantry brigades would then advance parallel to the main road; 8 Canadian Infantry Brigade (comprising Le Régiment de la Chaudière and Queen's Own Rifles of Canada) would be north of the road while 9 Canadian Infantry Brigade (including the Glengarry Highlanders and North Nova Scotia Highlanders) would be to the south. If all went to plan, the 8 Infantry Brigade would then clear the area around Wimereux and 9 Infantry Brigade would clear the Outreau peninsular

The initial attack went well with Kangaroo personnel carriers swiftly transporting infantry to where they were most needed along the front line. 8 Brigade lost no time in taking the Rupembert radar station intact and set up a forward command post at Marlborough just a mile from the city centre. 9 Brigade had a tougher time of things but once elements of the 79th Armoured Division had cleared several routes through minefields, their

Heights above Boulogne looking north towards Gris Nez.

AVREs and Churchill Crocodile flame-throwing tanks were able to link up with those of the Fort Garry Horse and the key strategic heights of Mont Lambert were mostly in Canadian hands by nightfall on the first day of the battle for Boulogne.

There had been genuine fears that the battery at La Tresorerie would severely hamper Allied operations but its garrison was too busy attempting to hold off the North Shore Regiment to fire its big guns and, despite getting trapped in a minefield at one point, the Canadians had disabled the battery by the time darkness fell on the second day. Meanwhile, the other two regiments in 8 Brigade were now making progress through the suburbs to the north of the city.

On the morning of the third day of the siege, 9 Brigade's North Nova Scotias finally gained overall control of Mont Lambert, at once rendering any long-term defence of Boulogne almost impossible. The Glengarry Highlanders, supported by AVREs, then attacked the ancient citadel in which many of the remaining German units had taken refuge. Its massive medieval walls were surrounded by a deep ditch and the Canadians feared they would have to launch a potentially costly frontal assault to break in. However, just as the AVREs were being prepared to move forward, a French civilian came forward and said he knew of a secret tunnel by which a platoon could gain access to the citadel without the Germans knowing.

He proved true to his word and, under the cover of an AVRE assault on the main gate, a group of Canadian infantry slipped

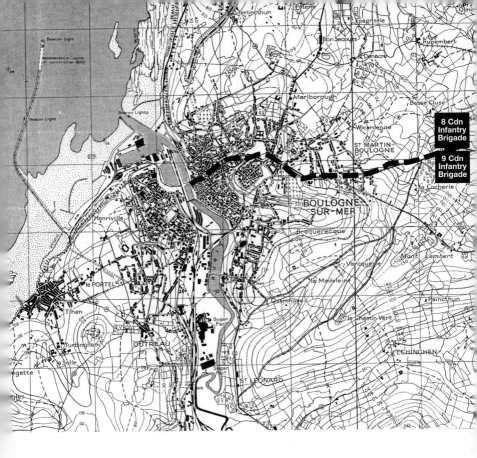

under the walls and cut off a German retreat. The defenders quickly threw down their arms.

Supported by specialist armour, a company of North Nova Scotias managed to reach the River Liane in the city centre where their ranks were quickly swelled by the Highland Light Infantry of Canada. The bridges had been partially destroyed by retreating Germans but improvised repairs were made on one bridge overnight and by the third day, some transport had been able to cross the river in support of the infantry

There was no stopping the Canadians now and once over the Liane, 9 Brigade moved south along the river's west bank and the Glengarry Highlanders took the suburb of Outreau despite coming under heavy shelling from a fortified position on top of the peninsular between the river and the sea. The Cameron Highlanders of Ottawa successfully completed their assault on Herquelingue heights, east of the river, overnight on 18 September

S-Boote safe in their individual concrete bays in Boulogne harbour.

The same pens after constant raids by RAF Bomber Command.

but then encountered a German force that had been hiding out in tunnels underneath the fortifications. They were supported by armour from the 79th Armoured Division.

Outside the Citadel, which was surrounded by a high wall and had only two gates, an infantry company was held up by machine gun fire. A Sherman commanded by Sergeant Grant, Lothians, located and destroyed four gun positions on its walls while the rest of the column entered the market-square where they were greeted by white flags and Lieutenant Sloan of B column.

The advance guard made for the river, and other tanks for the Citadel gate where three mines were removed and two Shermans entered. They were not the first to arrive; the two AVREs left to support the company pinned by machine-gun fire, petarded the main gate and demolished the rails which blocked it. At this moment white flags appeared on the battlements and the Adjutant came out with thirty men to arrange surrender. The AVREs helped to round up two to three hundred prisoners.

In the north, the North Shore Regiment had moved on the coastal resort of Wimereux, while the Queen's Own Rifles and the Chaudière regiment moved against the heavily-defended Fort de la Creche. By the fifth day, both objectives had been achieved with the latter surrendering following an intense bombing raid by the RAF

Fort de la Creche casemate with 37 mm Flak gun and a defending 75 mm field gun. A wrecked staff car can be seen alongside the gun.

Crocodile flame-throwers encouraged the German defenders to surrender.

and a further bombardment by artillery.

Boulogne was almost totally now under Allied control but the Germans continued to hold out at Le Portel on the Outreau peninsular. An ultimatum was delivered by loud speakers to its defenders and the garrison marched out to surrender. General Heim and the last vestiges of the Boulogne garrison were left alone in the last remaining strongpoint in the south of the city, but still they kept firing. Backed up against the harbour walls, the Germans had nowhere to go so heavy armour, including flame-throwers, was brought forward to persuade them to surrender. It did the trick, and the Germans destroyed their guns and General Heim led his men out under a white flag. Only Calais and Dunkerque now stood between the Canadians and the Belgian border.

CALAIS

Opposite the Kent coast, the coastline of the Pas de Calais was the most heavily defended section of the Atlantic Wall. There are far too many anti-tank walls, gun emplacements, bunkers and turrets to list and many of the fortifications were simply abandoned as the Allied forces swept up from the south and along the coast, cutting off German forces in the process. But, thanks to the book *The Story of the 79th Armoured Division*, national military archives and various regimental diaries, it is possible to piece together how some of the more formidable batteries were over-run and what became of the defences.

The Pas de Calais was the epicentre of the Atlantic Wall, from which the line of fortifications stretched hundreds of kilometres to both north and south, from the Pyrenees to the Arctic Circle. Here was where the Germans awaited the Allied invasion they knew would one day come. But it was August 1944, after the Allies were already firmly established on French soil, before British and Canadian forces began to engage defenders. By this time, any threat of an effective counter-attack by Hitler's forces had already receded and it was a question of not 'if' but 'when' would Calais and Dunkerque be liberated.

The Canadian North Shore Regiment had endured a particularly torrid journey since landing on JUNO Beach. Involved in the costly Battle of Falaise Gap, by 8 August the regiment received orders to move up to the frontline behind the armour which was trying to break through German lines. A message was passed on saying that the advance was not going as rapidly as planned and that they were to hold up in the area of Cormelles.

After finding a suitable battalion area, the company reconnaissance parties broke down into teams. But before a plan of action could be formulated, the vanguard saw a wall of fire and smoke coming towards them across the valley. Too stunned to initially react, they only just managed to dive into a trench before the concussion from multiple explosions ripped open the ground around them. Most of the reconnaissance party had managed to get under cover and had suffered no damage with the exception of their jeeps, which were completely wrecked. But casualties among the rest of the regiment were appalling. The North Shore suffered thirty-seven fatalities and seventy eight wounded. They had been hit by two squadrons of American B17 Flying Fortresses that had lost their bearings over the English Channel and dropped their load on what they perceived to be retreating German forces.

The North Shore regiment could do little but regroup and press on, however, and by September 1944 they were on the outskirts of Calais.

Operation UNDERGO

The Calais area was the only point from where the British ports of Dover and Folkestone could be shelled by German cross-channel guns and where the invasion of Fortress Europe would be most likely, due to the proximity of Britain's shoreline. The defences here, therefore, were immense by any standard; the guns housed in re-inforced concrete emplacements were the most powerful available at that time. But these defences were prepared to counter an invasion from the sea and, had it not been for local commanders, the landward side would have been almost totally undefended. Operation UNDERGO, the operation to nullify the guns of the Pas De Calais, had much in its favour therefore – but Allied generals knew their men could take nothing for granted even though many of the batteries' garrisons were not front-line troops.

The batteries in the area around Cap Gris Nez were among the most imposing. Four 380 mm guns were housed at *Batterie Todt*, parts of which are still preserved and serve as a part of the Atlantic

At the beginning of the war, Pointe Gris Nez was equipped with a battery of two 240 mm Skoda K16 guns which were later replaced by pieces of 170 mm calibre seen here.

German officers scrutinize the English coast at the foot of the lighthouse at Gris Nez.

Wall Museum at Audinghen. The battery was originally to have been called *Batterie Siegfried* but was renamed in honour of the founder after he was mysteriously killed in a plane crash in 1942. The Floringzelle area housed the *Batterie Grosser Kürfurst* (this translates as 'Great Elector'), a battery of four 280 mm guns with an all-round traverse, while *Batterie Wissant*, further to the east had other guns of 150 mm calibre, pointing into the English Channel. These were all dwarfed, however, by the 406 mm guns of the Batterie *Lindemann* at Sangatte. All of these batteries had heavy anti-aircraft defences consisting of the 88 mm and 20 mm guns, most of which were to be converted for the defence of the perimeter of Calais and Cap Gris Nez. The cross-channel gun emplacements were not entirely devoid of landward defences: anti-tank ditches – some of them concealed – minefields, razor wire and concrete bunkers all ringed the fortifications but, as elsewhere on the Atlantic Wall, there was little co-ordination. Their garrison of *Kriegsmarine* troops was also a strong factor, which influenced the efficiency of these defences when the Allies began encircling the area.

The wide range of targets, the delay in getting to Antwerp caused by reducing them by force and the estimated cost were also causes of Montgomery's early decision to encircle but not reduce Calais and Dunkerque was prompted by the need to reach Antwerp as soon as possible. These two ports were left to wither on the vine. However, after the capture of the port of Boulogne, the Royal Navy expressed concerns about shelling of the Channel traffic by the coastal batteries in the area, which could deny the Allies the free use of Boulogne.

By noon 5 September 1944, elements of the 7th Canadian Reconnaissance Regiment and the 3rd Canadian Infantry Division succeeded in containing the garrisons of the area, 7 Canadian Infantry Brigade arrived later from Boulogne to assist with the encirclement and containment. Gathering of intelligence data started immediately, sourcing information from the interrogation of prisoners of war and local civilians. One of the locals actually brought a complete map of the defences around Sangatte that fleeing Germans had left behind.

The German line of defences, where the Canadian advance was

Approaches to the port of Calais as they were in the 1940s.

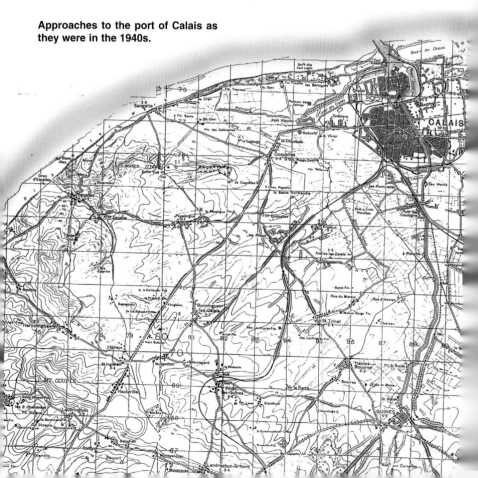

stopped or diverted, was based on flooded low ground as no high features similar to those around Boulogne were in the vicinity. Defenders were also aided by natural features such as canals or dykes (the city of Calais was built on a series of islands), strongly defended or covered by artillery or small arms fire from pre-planned outposts.

Oberstleutnant Ludwig Schroeder was later found to be in command of the garrison, but after his capture, his interrogators reported that he was found to be a 'mediocre and accidental' leader, who was charged with commanding the area only because he happened to be the most senior officer around. Schroeder had been in the Calais area since 30 August 1944, when Hitler was only starting to realize the invasion for which he was waiting had already taken place at Normandy nearly three months earlier.

First attempts to close in on the defences were made on 12 and 13 September 1944, but were opposed by furious artillery shelling, and the Allied demand for surrender was rejected.

Despite plans to begin the assault earlier, it was not possible due to various reasons, including the prolonged siege of Boulogne, to commence operations around Calais before 25 September 1944. For days, the German garrison was being pounded by Allied shelling from strong artillery formations, which had been brought over after the completion of Operation WELLHIT. These units had to be brought in under a huge smoke screen to block them from view of the German observers. This smoke screen lasted for six days, pausing only for air bombardment, using up 147 tons of smoke generators. The assault itself went on in much the same way as before at Le Havre or Boulogne, with the 79th Armoured Division making gaps in the defences, while 7 and 8 Canadian Infantry Brigades followed on foot. By noon the next day, the Sangatte battery had been captured along with the battery commander and 280 of his men. In the evening of 26 September, the Canadians had captured twenty-eight officers and 1,525 other ranks. The early capture of

Calais from the high ground inland.

Sangatte effectively cut the perimeter in half, causing the two flanks to become separate thrusts rather than a united offensive.

The prolonged siege of Boulogne had delayed forces arriving at Calais and full operations around the port didn't commence until 25 September. For days, the German garrison was being pounded by Allied shelling from land and sea, the land-based artillery having been brought over after the completion of Operation WELLHIT at Boulogne. These units had to be brought in under a huge smoke screen to block them from view of the German observers. Canadians made up the majority of the Allied forces. This smoke screen lasted for almost six days, pausing only for an RAF air bombardment, and used up almost 150 tons of smoke generators.

Crossing the canals of Calais proved to be a formidable task and once they had been crossed, troops faced the danger of being cut off from the main force. Two companies of the 1st Battalion Canadian Scottish Regiment were to suffer this fate in the western part of the city. A large number of civilians were still trapped in the city so a truce was arranged in the morning of 29 September to arrange their evacuation. This brought rather peculiar problems. But the only transport available was German trucks and many of the truck drivers themselves refused to go back into the city and insisting on being taken prisoner. Despite some initial concerns that accepting their requests could constitute a breach in the conditions of the truce, the Allies obliged and the end was in sight for Calais' garrison.

Another meeting of Allied and German officers took place, creating some confusion as *Oberstleutnant* Schroeder offered to surrender two hours after the truce was supposed to end. This was rejected by the Canadians who renewed hostilities as soon as the truce ended but the Germans had obviously had enough and began to lay down their arms as the Allies advanced towards their lines. The official German surrender was accepted from Schroeder's hands on the evening of 30 September.

Outside the city, the capture of Cap Gris Nez had developed into an equally arduous operation and the German garrisons ensconced in heavily-defended batteries dotted along the coastal road seemingly had no intention of surrendering without a fight.

Batterie Grosser Kurfürst

The 79th Armoured Division used Crocodiles, Crabs and AVREs in the initial attack on *Batterie Grosser Kursfürst* was mounted following an artillery barrage laid down by one field regiment, two medium regiments and two heavy artillery batteries. More than 1,000 rounds were fired during the operation which was directed by Air Observation Posts. The railway guns at St Margaret's in Kent weighed in with sixty-eight rounds of their own and and managed to damage all four guns of the *Batterie Grosser Kurfürst* on Cap Gris-Nez to varying degrees. Bomber

Batterie Grosser Kurfurst which, unlike the other batteries, could traverse its four gun turrets 360 degrees enabling them to fire inland.

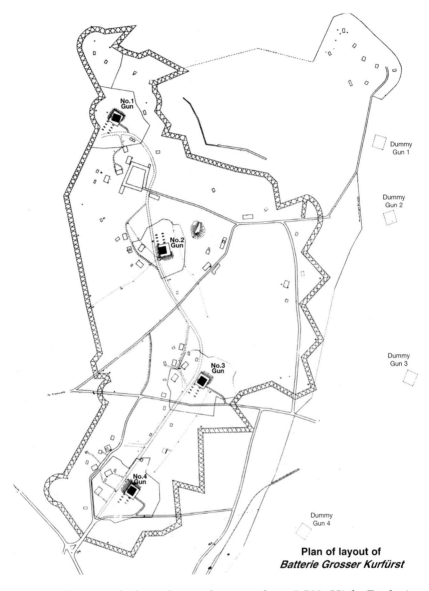

Plan of layout of
Batterie Grosser Kurfürst

Command then dropped more than 3,500 High Explosive bombs, and Typhoons aircraft launched rockets at the site.

When the actual ground assault started, a considerable number of the 79th Armoured Division's specialized armour was lost to mines or got bogged down in the craters created by the air bombardment. Only a single flail tank got far enough to force a gap in the minefields for the infantry. But 9 Brigade, with armoured support from the 1st Hussars (6th Armoured Regiment) and Crocodile flame-throwing tanks and AVREs from the 79th Armoured Division, had been deployed to Cap Gris-Nez so the Allies wouldn't be short of firepower against the region's big batteries. The Highland Light Infantry of Canada would attack the two northern batteries, the *Grosser Kurfürst* and Gris Nez itself, while the North Nova Scotia Highlanders attacked *Batterie Todt* (at Haringzelles).

An accurate bombardment from British heavy guns at Dover (Winnie and Pooh) had proved so effective that the *Batterie Grosser Kurfürst* which, unlike the other batteries, could traverse 360 degrees and was capable of bombarding Allied forces inland was quickly put out of action.

The British long-range artillery, which started firing at 6:35 am on 29 September, continued with a creeping barrage that successfully kept German defenders pinned down until the Canadian infantry was on top of them. Once breached, German positions quickly surrendered and *Grosser Kurfurst* had surrendered in its entirety by 10:30 am. The smaller Gris Nez was taken with relatively few casualties during the afternoon. If anything, the North Nova Scotia Highlanders encountered even less resistance, reaching the actual gun emplacements without any

No.1 gun of *Batterie Grosser Kurfürst* after its capture.

opposition whatsoever. The reinforced concrete walls had proved too thick, even for AVRE petards fired at close range, with one officer commenting that it was like trying to make a hole in a barrel of beer with a pea shooter. But the noise and concussion of hand grenades thrown into embrasures persuaded the Germans to surrender *en masse*. The local German HQ at Cran-aux-Oeufs also capitulated without a struggle.

The Canadians lost three officers with five deaths among other ranks. The Germans lost twenty-six officers with 1,500 other ranks captured. On capture, the German garrison was found to know very little of what was going on outside their bunkers.

BATTERIE LINDEMANN

The final approach to Calais under the giant smoke screen had allowed the North Shore Regiment to get close to the *Batterie Lindemann* at Sangatte. A large sand model had been constructed so that everyone would know exactly what to do when facing the formidable guns named *Anton*, *Bruno* and *Caesar*, the first three letters of the phonetic alphabet favoured by the German military

The battery was named after Ernst Lindemann, who the year before had perished as captain of the battleship *Bismarck*. The three 406 mm Adolf guns were taken from the *Batterie Schleswig Holstein* in Poland. The guns, firing a 1300 lb shell, had a range of thirty-five miles and were the most powerful in the Pas de Calais. It could also fire a 2250 lb grenade with a range of twenty-six miles and the

Batterie Lindemann under construction.

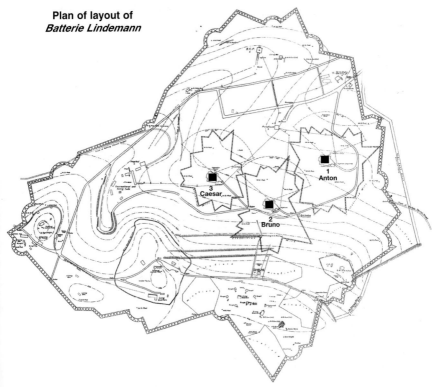

sixty-five-foot barrel could manage between 250 and 300 shots before it needed re-boring. The guns were mounted in individual bunkers which were cast in reinforced concrete that measured up to four metres thick in places. The guns shelled south-east England regularly and, in the two years they were operational, over 2,200 shots landed in Kent.

Batterie Lindemann, therefore, proved a popular target for the Allies during their bombing raids. Allied bombs had no effect on the large bunkers, however, but on 4 September, 1944, an artillery shell from an English railway gun based near Dover, passed straight through the embrasure of *Bruno* and a week later, a bomb-aimer had a similar stroke of good fortune and destroyed *Caesar*.

The Canadian infantry was to hammer the final nail into the coffin of *Batterie Lindemann* and with the help of the tanks from the 79th Armoured Division, the North Shore was able to quickly over-run the outer trenches and the garrison retreated back towards its bunkers.

This AVRE belonged to 284 Assault Squadron, Royal Engineers. Descending the steep slope behind Lindemann Batterie it ended up alongside this blockhouse which served as the reserve magazine A.

Progress was halted towards the guns themselves, however, when the Flails had trouble in the minefields particularly on the right hand bank where they were trying to use the new Conger (an explosive hose attached to a rocket) to clear a path. One luckless tank crew even overbalanced over the edge of an embrasure it had failed to see in the smoke and ended up in front of one of the huge guns on its side. But by noon B Company had reached the left-hand crest with D Company less one platoon right behind. They were still having trouble getting down the seaward slope, however, as the Germans had only given up the crest so they could concentrate accurate machine-gun fire from their remaining positions.

British 8 Brigade also found the gun positions at Sangattes/Noires Mottes to be formidable: machine guns, wire, mines, an anti-tank ditch and the naturally steep slope protecting positions and making it difficult for armour to get close enough to threaten the battery's outer defences.

The diary of the 79th Armoured Division reported Crabs of C

Casemate Bruno of _Batterie Lindemann_ showing a crafty ruse of camouflage – a gun has been painted on the side to draw fire against an impenetrable wall should the position be attacked from the air, land or sea. Below: Canadian North Shore troops after capturing the gun.

Squadron, 1st Lothians & Border Yeomanry, led the way up from the south. Two troops flailed a narrow lane, under fire support from the rest of the Squadron and Canadian tanks, between the craters

Impressive size of casemate 'Caesar' with its turret and 406 mm gun.

and almost to the position itself. There they were stuck and a Conger was brought forward and fired. Meanwhile the third troop went with Captain E. March, Royal Engineers, to the West where craters were fewer. A lane was cleared, exploding some thirty-five mines and cutting through two double apron wire fences. Infantry followed by the Crabs, AVREs and some Crocodiles, got through this gap and the one made by the Conger and took the forward position.

The rest of the feature was no easier to take, the ridge being constantly shelled by long-range field guns in Calais and at Battery Gris-Nez. The guns were, of course, out of range to the tanks but they did succeed in knocking out an 88 mm on the beach below.

To encourage the infantry, Captain March started off with a mixed force of tanks. His AVRE led the way down the steep slope, but after about 200 yards fell over the edge of a blockhouse and turned turtle. Cratering was very bad and a Crocodile lost its trailer on a mine. A second Crocodile had its trailer hit four times and a third lost a track to direct hits from an 88mm position – the advance petered out.

As darkness fell, however, infantry officers returned and reported that they had taken eighteen prisoners and found a large concrete warehouse built into the hillside, two ammunition bunkers full of small arms and a complete underground hospital. A larger group retraced the officers' steps and found another ammunition bunker occupied by twenty Germans, who also surrendered. They then moved on to the hospital. The telephone system from the hospital to the main bunkers was out so they used a less-seriously injured patient as a runner to carry an ultimatum to surrender at first light or face the consequences. The runner, while looking for the commandant, visited other bunkers and spread the message around.

Dawn revealed a sea of white flags. One by one the bunkers were surrendering and by the next morning, the North Shore was in complete possession of the Pas de Calais' most fearsome battery.

What the bombs and shells of the Allies had struggled to destroy, the Channel Tunnel managed to achieve at the end of the 20th century. Engineering works at the tunnel entrance in Sangatte formed a huge lake which submerged most of the *Batterie Lindemann* and only a few scattered walls and bunkers now remain above the water.

BATTERIE TODT

Batterie Todt was opened in a ceremony attended by *Kriegsmarine* Admirals Raeder and Dönitz 20 January 1942 but wasn't officially commissioned until 10 February 1942. Initially named *Batterie Siegfried*, it was renamed in honour of the Todt Organisation's founder Fritz Todt who had been killed in a mysterious plane crash a month earlier. Two days later, on 12

February the battery went into action, providing covering fire for the battleships *Gneisenau* and *Scharnhorst* and heavy cruiser *Prinz Eugen* who were attempting to make their way through the English Channel into the northern Atlantic.

The battery site is located south of Cap Gris-Nez at Haringzelle. It was capable of firing shells up to forty-two kilometres from its elevated altitude of between sixty and seventy metres on cliffs and frequently targeted the Kent coast and Dover in particular 25 miles away. The battery's guns were protected by reinforced concrete casemates and surrounded by minefields, anti-aircraft batteries and searchlights. In addition, a ring of eight machine gun Tobruks guarded the landward side along with anti-tank guns and razor wire.

Eighteen enlisted men were overseen by four officers in each of the four *Türme* or towers which housed the guns, while the battery was directed by a radar station and observation post at nearby Cran-aux-Oeufs, where a further 600 men were on standby to help with coastal defence should an attack take place. The battery saw significant offensive action in 1942 but its firing became more selective in 1943 and, by the time of the Allied invasion, ammunition had become so scarce that the guns were only fired

Observation post and fire control at nearby Cran-aux-Oeufs.

when a specific target had been identified.

Batterie Todt formed part of the 242nd Coast Artillery Battalion commanded by Lieutenant Commander Kurt Schilling, who was also responsible for *Batterie Lindemann, Batterie Grosser Kürfurst* and the *Batterie Gris Nez*, but the beginning of the end of its operational life came about on 29 September, 1944 when the 3rd Canadian Infantry Division arrived in the area having fought their way up from Normandy. The garrisons of Boulogne and Calais were already teetering on the brink and those defending *Batterie Todt*, at that time under the command of *Fähnrich* Klaus Mombera, knew their turn wasn't far away and commented after the war:

> *The bunkers were protected by minefields and anti-tank support points that we had installed in a hurry. Machine guns and field guns recovered from retreating troops were gathered around the area of Cap Gris Nez and we had 1,800 sailors and soldiers prepared to make a last stand.*

On 26 September the RAF had launched 532 bombers in a raid on Cap Gris Nez, which dropped 855 tonnes of bombs inside three hours. On the ground, the North Nova Scotia Highlanders had been charged with taking and disabling *Batterie Todt*. Led by the charismatic Lieutenant-Colonel DF Forbes and spearheaded by B Squadron of the 6th Armoured Regiment as well as the flail-tanks, Crocodiles and AVREs of the British 79th Armoured Division, the assault began at 6.45 pm and by 10.30 pm, white flags were flying above the *Batterie Todt*. In a final gesture of defiance, No. 2 *Turm* fired a final shell at Dover as the Canadian troops swarmed over its roof and abseiled into the embrasure – the gun finally fell silent.

No. 3 *Turm* had been destroyed by the bombing on 26 September and No 4 *Turm*, partly hidden in woods, offered little resistance when its occupants saw *Turm* 1 and *Turm* 2 being overrun. The garrison at Cran-aux-Oeufs surrendered shortly after.

ATLANTIC WALL MUSEUM

Turm 1 now houses the Atlantic Wall Museum, which has examples of weapons, ammunition and information about the battery and others in the area. *Turm 2* is located in woods nearby, and has been sealed to preserve the interior while the remains of *Turm 3* were largely demolished after the war. *Turm 4* is located at the edge of a farmer's field and remains in good condition. Other bunkers located in the woods around the battery remain open to investigation where they have been deemed safe.

BATTERIE OLDENBURG

Batterie Oldenburg was built just to the east of Calais. Remnants can be seen from the main ring road to the ferry ports as it's located beyond the sand dunes near the former Seacat and Hoverspeed terminal. The battery featured two 210 mm guns mounted in casemates known as *Turm Ost* (East) and *Turm West*.

The impressive 240 mm gun SKC/40 at Marine *Batterie Oldenburg*.

The gun emplacements had the standard two levels and included storerooms and accommodation. *Turm Ost* remains in good conditions for its age but the interior of *Turm West* was torn apart by an explosion which destroyed most of the floor beneath the gun and many of the rooms behind. Visitors to the site can still gain safe entry to other bunkers, however, including the observation and fire command post and the battery hospital.

BATTERIE FRIEDRICH AUGUST

The *Batterie Friedrich August* can be found near the small town of La Trèsorerie, north of Boulogne. The battery was declared operational on August 15 1940 under leadership of *Kapitan* Franz Diekmann and had a garrison that totalled more than 400 in its heyday. Three 305 mm Krupp/Skoda guns were situated in open emplacements and had a range of between thirty-two and fifty-one kilometres, depending on the weight of the shell being fired. Later on, the large guns were placed in concrete emplacements to protect them against bombing. The 240th M.A.A. battery also consisted of numerous flak, Tobruks and other defensive positions. It was attacked by 8 Canadian Infantry Brigade, 17 September 1944. One day later the battery surrendered. Only one casemate, *Turm* 2, can be visited. The front of the bunker, where the gun was placed is completely destroyed but the back can be entered and many rooms on the two levels are still intact. On the ground floor, plenty of German graffiti is still visible. *Turm* 3 completely disappeared and only ruins are left of *Turm* 1.

Batterie Friedrich August shortly after its capture.

German defenders at Wissant: top, emplacement for a 50 mm gun. Above, anti tank wall.

WISSANT

An eerie graveyard of defensive positions and bunkers that have slipped onto the beach due to coastal erosion. The stakes that supported both *Teller* mines and barbed wire are still in place but local authorities have now closed off most of the site and beach due to safety fears. Demolition has been scheduled and this remarkable monument to Second World War engineering will be lost forever in the next few years.

DUNKERQUE

By the time the Germans finally surrendered Dunkerque to a largely Canadian and Czech force on 8 May 1944, Allied forces already had established supply routes onto the European mainland largely through the port of Antwerp.

On 15 September 1944, the 4, 5 and 6 Infantry Brigades of the 2nd Canadian Infantry Division were ordered to be stood down. They'd fought their way from Normandy to the very tip of northern France. By 18 September, the Canadians had moved on to advance towards Antwerp while the containment of Dunkerque was assigned to 4 South Saskatchewan Brigade. This unit was, in turn, relieved within nine days by 51st Highland Infantry Division, coming under the direct command of First Canadian Army.

On 6 October, the Czechoslovak Independent Armoured Brigade Group was deployed around the perimeter, together with formations of British, Canadian and French troops, completing the relief of 154 Highland Infantry Brigade by 9 October 1944. Major-General Alois Liska, the commanding officer of the Czech Brigade Group, was given overall command and the whole of the perimeter and the surrounding area fell under his jurisdiction.

Other Allied formations involved in the siege included the 2nd Canadian Heavy Anti-aircraft Regiment and 109th Heavy Anti-Aircraft Regiment, Royal Artillery, equipped with 40 mm Bofors guns and 125th Light Anti-aircraft Regiment also with Bofors guns. The anti-aircraft formations were experienced in offensive infantry support by firing air-burst H.E. rounds, a practice successfully

Montegomery and Major-General Alois Liska, the commanding officer of the Czech Brigade Group which was tasked with containing the Germans within Dunkerque.

A 3.7 inch anti-aircraft gun being dragged into position during siege of Dunkerque.

employed at Calais and Boulogne. The 7th Royal Tank Regiment, engaged previously in Operation ASTONIA, was deployed in the westernmost part of the port's perimeter, guarding its section outlined by the Channel coast on one side and the road from Dunkerque to Loon-Plage on the other.

The town of Loon-Plage was made the Field Artillery Regiment's HQ and its two batteries, each with four 25-pounder field guns were based there during the entirety of the siege of Dunkerque.

South of the road, the Czechoslovak 1st Armoured Regiment under the command of Major Rezabek controlled a sector that stretched down to the Canal de Bourbourg. The Czechs were equipped with Cromwell cruiser tanks as well as close support Cromwell CS (close support) tanks mounting 95mm howitzers. They also had Crusader anti-aircraft tanks and later Challenger and Sherman Firefly tank killers armed with 17-pounder anti-tank guns. The unit was a continuation of the Czechoslovak 1st Infantry Division in France and the 1st Infantry Battalion of the Czechoslovak Independent Brigade in Britain.

The Free French had two infantry battalions under the command of Lieutenant-Colonel Lehagre and supported the Czechs which also featured an Armoured Reconnaissance Squadron under Major Velimsky.

145

Dunkerque was all about containment and to that end a Field Engineers Company equipped with dinghies with outboard motors maintained regular patrols between houses and farms in outlying areas to ensure the Germans weren't being resupplied by land. At sea, a Czech Motor Battalion's boats swept the English Channel to turn back German E-boats bringing supplies and orders to the port now completely cut off from any kind of command or support.

Atlantic Wall fortifications in Dunkerque had suffered badly in bombing raids in comparison with some of the other *Festunghäfe* ports and for that reason this book won't be delving in-depth into its eventual liberation. But the city proved to be among the most difficult to liberate as the Germans took literally Hitler's order to fight to the last man and much of the port was razed to the ground in bloody hand-to-hand street fighting until General Liska finally accepted the German garrison's unconditional surrender from the hands of *Vizeadmiral* Frisius on 8 May, 1945. Dunkerque was to be the last French city to be liberated.

General De Gaulle and the Free French government had disagreed with any suggestion to subject Dunkerque to extensive air or naval bombardment, which was essential for the success of previous operations in festung ports earlier that year. Also, the Canadian and later the Czechoslovak troops overseeing containment would have been totally outnumbered and outgunned and the advantage of tanks and armoured vehicles in the area was negligible.

The surrounded port was to be contained, not taken, as the estimated casualties did not match with the target's importance. The Brigade Group's mission was to contain the German troops and influence their determination to fight on by aggressive reconnaissance activities. Counter-invasion measures, although largely useless after June 1944, were applied all along the coast.

Anti-aircraft batteries were also still operational, often including medium and heavy anti-aircraft artillery, and mines were deployed in their thousands, particularly in the eastern part of the perimeter, north of the Canal de Dunkerque and east of the heavily fortified Fort des Dunes. The cemetery to the southeast of the Rosendael Hospital, where the British memorial now stands, was also mined as was the road bypassing it. As the Czechoslovak engineers would learn during some of the attacks of the siege, at some places three or four *Teller* mines were found on top of each other in the ground. Electrically-triggered explosive charges were also common.

146

The centre of the city had obvious advantages for the defenders. Canals divided the city into easily defendable sectors, one creating a natural obstacle blocking the access to the city centre, where the German headquarters was located. The canal banks were lined with trenches, strongpoints, improvised pillboxes and bridges could be easily destroyed to delay an advance. Streets were blocked by road blocks and barricades built up from the debris.

A POW camp was also located in the city centre, with prisoners of war held at the town prison in Rue des Ramparts next to the Quai De La Citadelle. About sixty British and Canadian soldiers were held during the siege, together with members of the French Resistance and two downed American Air Force NCOs, one of whom was blown out of the rear turret of a B17 bomber into a mine field.

The inland part of the port's perimeter was also heavily defended. As in Normandy and parts of the Pas de Calais, the low country surrounding Dunkerque had been flooded by the Germans by opening the locks on the coast, the high level of water being maintained by allowing a flow into artificial lakes during high tide. The Germans, well-accustomed to the features of the local terrain, exploited every possibility to support their defensive works. Houses, farms and non-essential factories in the suburbs and the surrounding countryside were transformed into strongpoints and and pre-built bunkers installed before D-Day were also re-commissioned.

Vizeadmiral Friedrich Frisius.

There were 25,000 civilians trapped in the port when the Canadians began to tighten the noose, though 6,000 did manage to leave the city either secretly or during a truce arranged by the Red Cross on 20 September. By 5 October, the majority of those remaining had managed to escape the hardship of what had become know locally as 'The Pocket' so by the time of the Czech take-over, only 820 civilians remained within the city and another 145 (mostly children, the old and the sick), left the city as late as 18 April 1945, during yet another truce.

Even after the arrival of the Czechs, the Allies still had no idea who they were dealing with inside Dunkerque. *Leutnantgeneral* von Kluge was reportedly in the port when it was surrounded and his signature was on a written rejection of a request by the Canadians for the surrender of the German garrison. But over the winter of 1944-45, he apparently escaped from the port by boat and was replaced by *Vizeadmiral* Friedrich Frisius, the former commander of the Pas de Calais. *Oberst* von Wittstadt became his chief of staff, while *Hauptmann* Schneider remained in the position of the commanding officer of the port installations of Dunkerque. *Major* Turke was also a key figure in organising the defences.

German military strength in the port was impressive, despite their hopeless position, but the quality of the troops was dubious. When the garrison surrendered at 9.20 am on 8 May 1945, there were 354 officers and 10,884 soldiers divided into five battle groups and twenty-one battalions. A further 542 wounded and 141 sick were found at the Rosendael Hospital. The troops were an eclectic mix of *Heer, Waffen-SS, Luftwaffe, Kriegsmarine* and *Festungspionere* units, including the 226th Infantry Division, 346th, 711th, 49th and 97th Divisions and the 26th and 1046th Fortress Batalions. Most were remnants of infantry formations from Normandy or the Pas de Calais area, where the majority of their units had been lost during the Allied invasion and breakout. During the siege of the city, the Germans lost about 1,000 men and 890 more, including eighteen officers, were captured following the Czech take-over on 18 April, 1945.

What was a surprise was the amount of food found within Dunkerque when the war ended. More than twenty-one tons of provisions were uncovered and it is estimated that the garrison could have held out for a further three months without suffering shortages. The Germans also had 410 vehicles at their disposal, as well as 731 horse-pulled wagons and 998 horses. Three small submarines and seven other ocean-going craft were also captured. Incredibly, the Germans still had more than 133,000 individual pieces of ammunition and 85 artillery pieces ranging from 75 mm to 200mm cannons. There were also 97 anti-tank guns, small arms and 98,520 hand grenades.

Montgomery's decision to wait out the German surrender at Dunkerque appeared to be well-advised.

Chapter Seven

FORTRESS OR FOLLY? CONCLUSIONS

I
T IS ALMOST CERTAIN that the Atlantic Wall was intended to compensate for German military weakness in the West and ostensibly deter an Allied invasion rather than form an impenetrable barrier. Ultimately, Hitler and his generals knew that once the Wall was breached, very little stood in the way of an Allied advance to Berlin. There might have been a chance of repulsing the Normandy invasion had the *1st Panzer Korps*, based approximately 100 miles from Caen, and mobile heavy artillery been better situated or given permission to advance earlier. But a centralised and over-complex German communication structure and the fact that none of their senior commanders were in the vicinity lost the only chance the Nazi regime had to drive the Allies back into the sea and the window of opportunity was quickly closed.

In researching this book, I read somewhere that the Atlantic Wall 'took two years to build and two hours to breach. And once breached, the rest of it largely became redundant'. That is grossly over-simplifying both the construction of the Wall in France and the reasoning behind it. Putting aside politics, Germany's high command were not fools and, though under the control of what history accepts was a tyrant, they never intended that the Atlantic Wall would have the capability of repulsing the invasion on its own, merely that it bought time for

LIMITATIONS OF ATLANTIC WALL

DITTMAR ON LANDING POSSIBILITIES

Dittmar, the German military commentator, admitted last night that Germany's Atlantic Wall was not expected to prevent the allies from landing on the Continent, and invasion forces would have to be fought by defence in depth. "It must be admitted," he said, "that history has had examples of successful landings from the sea, in spite of the fact that a landing from the sea presents the utmost difficulties. Although our Atlantic Wall is a supreme structure, surpassing our Western Wall, and built on the same sound principles, we do not expect the might of a wall or the concrete of fortifications to be successful in beating off a landing attempt.

"The last and best must be done by the man himself. We have shown the strength of our defence in the east, frustrating Soviet attempts to break through. The British and Americans can rest assured that the same conception of defence in depth has been put into effect on the Channel and on the Atlantic coast.—*British United Press.*

149

Panzer reserves to move up from positions in the Seine valley and launch a co-ordinated counterattack. That plan may well have worked had Hitler, Rommel and von Runstedt not been trying to outmanoeuvre each other. After all, the US forces were penned down for several hours on OMAHA Beach and it was only the failure of the German armour to respond quickly enough that eventually allowed the Americans to move inland. It also should not be forgotten that most of the troops on the Atlantic Wall were either second-rate soldiers or *Ost* formations conscripted from Eastern Europe. The Russian Front had tied up many of Germany's elite fighting force.

Could the Germans have created more Panzer divisions with the steel used to reinforce strongpoints and battery bunkers on the Atlantic Wall? Probably, but would not those tanks have been sent east, where the immediate need was greatest, or west on the off-chance an invasion fleet would land somewhere along a largely indefensible coastline? Without the Atlantic Wall, the Allied invasion probably would have achieved all of its D-Day objectives with ease. The advance across France and into Germany was delayed much longer than anyone had envisaged by the courage and tenacity of those Germans left behind to defend the fortified Channel ports. They knew there was no hope of escape once surrounded but it took a prolonged campaign to finally open the ports such as Calais, Dunkerque and Le Havre to Allied shipping.

It could be argued, therefore, that Germany made the most of the resources it had at its disposal, however unpalatable that may appear to our modern sensibilities. Captured armaments were recycled as a matter of routine and slave labour and concrete was plentiful and cheap. Had German strategy matched the fortifications and more responsive tactics been employed, there may well have been a different outcome, as *Feldmarschal* von Rundstedt reflected on his capture. He lamented:

Had I been able to move the armoured divisions which I had behind the coast, I am convinced that the invasion would not have succeeded.

No *Luftwaffe* to protect the skies and interference from higher levels certainly played major roles in the defeat of the German Army after the Normandy invasion, according to von Rundstedt. But the former German commander-in-chief on the Western Front also admitted that he and his senior officers and

Von Rundstedt discusses what might have been if it had not been for...
with his American captors.

been outsmarted by the Allies and taken several decisions that were to compound their plight.

Von Rundstedt had surmised that the landings on OMAHA and UTAH and subsequent push up into the Cotentin Peninsula were merely a feint to distract from landings on either the Belgian coast or in the Pas De Calais farther west. By the time he and his subordinates realised that the 6 June invasion wasn't a false front, it was too late to save anything but the main reserve force of the German Army in France.

It was also alleged that interference from Berlin had wrecked earlier plans for the defence of France against invasion. Von Rundstedt knew there were not enough troops to cover the possible areas of invasion and also faced a constant battle to prevent those he had under his command being allocated to duties elsewhere. When he was finally given *carte blanche*, it was too late as the RAF and USAF had such overwhelming air superiority that they quickly reduced his reinforcements to tatters, cutting communications and destroying armour and established defensive positions.

The position on the ground immediately prior to D-Day was a shambles, Von Rundstedt admitted. He and former Chief of Staff, General Blumentritt, highlighted several basic weaknesses in the German defences. There was an inadequate number of troops to cover stretches of exposed coastline with gaps in the Atlantic Wall of up to thirty miles in places. The Wall itself was 'anything but a wall, just a bit of cheap bluff' according to von Rundstedt, and there was no organised reserve under central command to counterattack where the invasion came.

Von Rundstedt, like many other high-ranking German generals, said he did not have access to his country's most proficient troops. He complained bitterly that many of his best units had been sent on a 'fool's errand' to Italy, and throughout his command and after, he maintained the notion that it was,

> *Madness to continue the war in Italy that way. That frightful 'boot' of a country should have been evacuated. Mussolini should have been left where he was and we should have held a decent front with a few divisions on the Alpine frontier. They should not have taken away the best divisions from me in the West in order to send them to Italy.*

Of course, he had no way of knowing that German High Command was running out of troops on all fronts. 'Had I been able to move the armoured divisions which I had behind the coast, I am convinced that the invasion would not have succeeded.' he told the Americans, 'If I had been able to move the troops, then my air force would also have been in a position to attack hostile ships.'

Von Rundstedt revealed that his original plan would have been to ensure that the Allies would not have been able to sail their battleships close to shore so that they could engage the coastal batteries and forces would have sustained prohibitive losses during landing operations. To some extent, that happened at OMAHA but the British were able to come ashore with relative impunity on SWORD and the Canadians also made rapid inroads from JUNO. 'That was all a question of air force, air force, and again air force,' he commented.

Von Rundstedt wanted the landing beaches to resemble the disastrous Dieppe raid, only on a much larger scale, and remained adamant that the Allies would have had a much rougher ride had he been able to control his armoured divisions as he desired, 'We would certainly have been better off if a good many things had been different as regards the distribution of forces.' he reflected.

As for the Atlantic Wall itself, Von Rundstedt admitted it was a gamble that didn't pay off, 'The enemy probably knew more about it than we did ourselves,' he confessed, proclaiming the only wall that mattered in the Second World War was the one that ran from the Scheldt in Antwerp to the Seine in Paris, 'But further than that – one has only to look at it for one's self in Normandy to see what rubbish it was.'

With the exception of the fortress port of Cherbourg the Atlantic Wall in northern France, according to Von Rundstedt, merely consisted of a few pillboxes in holes in the sand so far apart that 'you needed field glasses to see the next one'. It was simply propaganda, he said, but admitted that the German people had believed it. He thought, however, that the Allies would have easily worked out its weaknesses because of their extensive air reconnaissance and the help of the local French Resistance.

Reflecting on the subject of German coastal batteries and artillery, the *Kriegsmarine* policy of mounting coastal guns as if they were on ships came in for particularly heavy criticism. It was undoubtedly a major design fault that the vast majority could fire only out to sea. Subsequently, they were of no use to land forces once encircled and the fact that most coastal batteries incorporated mainly captured guns meant it became increasingly difficult to keep them supplied with the correct ammunition.

Finally, von Rundstedt confessed that the Americans had totally caught him and his staff off guard by using the Cotentin Peninsula, and ultimately Cherbourg, as a giant beachhead. None of the German hierarchy could believe that the landings in Normandy were aimed primarily at securing a harbour. The route to the interior of France, after all, was three times as long from Cherbourg. Even as the Allies poured into the Cotentin Peminsula, most Germans still believed the major thrust would come through either Dunkerque or Antwerp and toward the Ruhr, which was why the troop concentrations were more compact in that sector and the fortifications more robustly constructed. The Cotentin, the German navy had assured field commanders, was only accessible at high tide and even then rocks and reefs below the water would wreak havoc on troop ships and landing craft. Of course, the Allies were to gain a further advantage by landing at low tide.

'We probably didn't know about the floating harbours.' Von Rundstedt admitted in explaining that the Germans had not considered Normandy as a likely landing area. 'I, at least, didn't. Whether the Navy knew of them I don't know.'

In June 1944, there were six or seven Panzer divisions in reserve but well spread out behind the front line in the west. Two were immediately available when the invasion started and two others were able to join the fray on the first day. Another one came from Belgium and a sixth was due to arrive from southern France. That arrived late, however, due to the action of the Resistance.

'The defensive role played by the armoured divisions near Caen during July and August was a great mistake,' Von Rundstedt confessed, 'but it was done on the orders of higher authority. We wanted to relieve the armoured divisions by infantry, but it was impossible in the bulge in front of Caen where they were also under fire from ships' guns. You can't relieve any troops then.'

Von Rundstedt's plan, which was rejected by Hitler, was to withdraw the armoured forces behind the River Orne to the east of Ouistreham, form up the reserve infantry and field artillery there, and then use the tanks as mobile units to attack the British and Canadian forces on the flanks. This option was backed up by the senior tank commander, General Geyr von Schweppenburg, but the armoured divisions were left where they were on the Führer's personal orders.

In conclusion, two vital factors led to the breaching of the Atlantic Wall and subsequently the success of the D-Day landings.

Firstly, there was the smashing of the main lines of military communication and transport, particularly the railway junctions. Available reserves couldn't be moved to the threatened areas and made the re-supply of armaments to batteries and strongpoints near impossible. The second factor was the attacks on road links and marching columns. This made it extremely difficult to move anything during daylight hours, and created bottlenecks of fuel and ammunition which could then be targeted by carpet bombing.

Senior Allied commanders were divided over the impact of this on German defences but Von Rundstedt said it had a profound effect on troops stationed on the Atlantic Wall in northern France. It also demoralized those reserves held in the rear. German planes by this time were outnumbered ten to one and any long-range reconnaissance had become 'absolutely nonexistent'. He was also scathing over the impact of 'Rommel's asparagus' which was planted with much fanfare as an effective defence against airborne invasion, but in many places was either covered by drifting sand or washed away by high tides.

So did the Atlantic Wall in Normandy and the Pas de Calais do what it was designed to do? On many levels, I believe the answer was in the affirmative. As a tool of propaganda, it reassured the

Field Marshal Gerd von Rundstedt, overseeing plans of the Atlantic Wall Construction.

A Propaganda poster in Dutch and the coastal fortification is depicted as a continuous line. It declares that 1943 will not be like 1918 when the Second Reich was forced to sign an armistice.

German civilian population that the Western Front was well protected. Likewise, it forced the Allies to take special measures to breach it. In the months prior to D-day, the cutting of supply lines by Allied air raids robbed the Atlantic Wall of the necessary materials required for further planned construction. Therefore, it can be argued that it would have presented an even more imposing barrier had all the defences originally planned been completed, and had those generals, with the authority to order reserves into action, not been absent or unwilling to act on D-day.

But the fact remains that once most sites had been circumvented and the allies had crossed the Seine, the situation was hopeless as far as the defenders were concerned, and thousands of German troops were sacrificed in the *Festunghäfe* ports with no hope of relief. There is probably some substance to the theory, therefore, that it wasn't the Atlantic Wall that failed, but those that planned their strategy around it.

Chapter Eight

ATLANTIC WALL SITES FEATURED

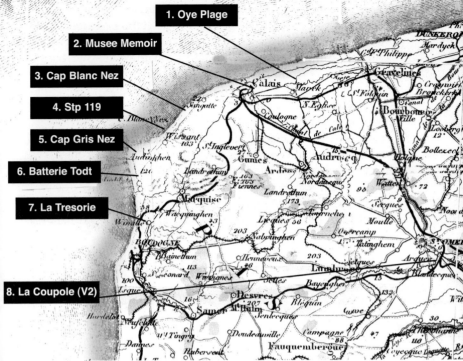

1. Oye Plage

2. Musee Memoir

3. Cap Blanc Nez

4. Stp 119

5. Cap Gris Nez

6. Batterie Todt

7. La Tresorie

8. La Coupole (V2)

1. OYE PLAGE

Remarkable for 'la tour penchee', a German Second World War observation post that was disguised as a church tower to confuse British air crews who used a nearby church tower as a navigation reference point. The beach adjoins the Platier D'Oye, a large nature reserve which was flooded in 1944 to combat possible Allied landings. An anti-tank wall which separates the wildlife reserve from sand dunes has several built-in machine-gun and anti-tank emplacements along its length.

Directions: From Calais, follow the D940 Route National east towards Gravelines. Oye Plage is approximetaly 7km beyond the turn for the Aeroport Calais-Dunquerque.

The Musée Mémoire in Calais housed in a former German communications bunker.

2. MUSÉE MÉMOIRE

Second World War museum located in the former German communications and operations centre in Calais. Features artifacts, documents, photographs and posters from the Second World War in a series of rooms.

Directions: Within easy walking distance of parking at the Calais Gare National or Calais Town Hall in a pleasant city park. Entrance signposted from the adjacent roundabout.

3. CAP BLANC NEZ

Capped by a monument to the maritime services, the site is surrounded by observation bunkers and firing posts from the Second World War and offers an excellent view of the white cliffs of Dover on a relatively clear day. There are many storage and personnel bunkers and Tobruks to explore off the beaten track, though caution must be exercised as some are in a perilous condition.

The walk to Cap Blanc Nez from the car parks can be quite arduous and may not be suitable for everyone but the site does offer a view across to the Channel Tunnel entrance at Sangatte and the giant man-made lake under which lies the remains of the formidable Batterie Lindemann.

4. WISSANT

One of the most remarkable and varied sites on the Atlantic Wall. Described as an 'elephants' graveyard' of Second World War relics the beach, behind an anti-tank wall, has an abundance of German bunkers that have been left high and dry by coastal erosion. The adjoining sand dunes also hide several installations associated with *Stp 119*. Nearby woods contain gun turrets and fortified emplacements.

Sadly, local authorities have deemed much of the area is now too dangerous for visitors and have closed off parts prior to demolition though the town is still well worth a visit.

Directions: From Calais, follow the D940 coast road west past Cap Blanc Nez and directions to Wissant are on the right. Alternatively, take the A16 and leave at junction 36. The D238 will take you directly to Wissant. There is plenty of free parking in the town.

Erosion has stranded these Atlantic Wall defences on the beach at Wissant.

StP		' StP 120 Pommern '	JPP	
		Dunes d'Aval, Wissant West	F1 2120 100B [F1 358]	
IGN 2103 ET CALAIS			1 : 2.500	01.07.2003

01 - Garage mit OB-LAG
02 - Regelbau 600
03 - Regelbau 630
04 - Tobruk in Pz.Mauer eingebaut
05 - Regelbau 501, angesprengt
06 - Regelbau 501
07 - Regelbau 502 mit Tobruk
08 - Schnabelstand, Trümmer
09 - Garage mit OB-LAG, 2002 entfernt
10 - Regelbau 612, gesprengt
11 - Panzermauer, fast vollständig umgekippt
12 - Plattform
13 - vermutlich Unterstand, heute nicht mehr vorhanden
14 - Tobruk in Panzermauer
15 - Regelbau 612, gesprengt
16 - OB für 50mm KwK
17 - Plattform, entfernt
18 - Panzermauerdurchlass
19 - MG-Stand
20 - MG-Stand
21 - unbekannt
22 - Unterschlupf
23 - unbekannt
24 - Regelbau 501 vermutet, gesprengt
25 - unbekannt
26 - unbekannt
27 - unbekannt
28 - Offene Bettung

Begehungen: 2001/2002/2003/2004/2005/2008

Diagram of Strongpoint 120, Wissant

5. CAP GRIS NEZ

Favourite viewing point for Nazi propaganda photographs of Dover's white cliffs. Heavily fortified point but defences would have been ineffective had the Allies invaded in the Pas de Calais.

Follow the D940 coast road from Calais through Wissant. Off-road parking is signposted in several places.

Oberservation bunker on Cap Gris Nez.

Personnel bunker with Ringstand attached.

6. Batterie Todt

SITUATED AT AUDINGHEN on Cap Gris Nez in the Pas de Calais, the **Batterie Todt** museum is housed in one of four original *Türme* or towers that comprised one of the most powerful gun batteries in the Pas de Calais during the Second World War.

On several well-maintained levels, there are gun rooms, an armoury, a hospital and troops' quarters housing an excellent private collection of German weapons, uniforms, ammunition and posters as well as several modes of military transport. Unfortunately, many of the exhibits aren't labelled and others are grouped together under a generic title which can be misleading. Arguably the complete Krupp 5 railway gun complete with chassis on a track at the side of the museum is worth the visit alone being only one of two known to survive Second World War.

Directions: Find the D940 towards Sangatte, by-passing Cap Blanc Nez and Wissant until you come to the crossroads with the D191. Take this road in the direction of Cap Gris Nez and almost immediately left. **Batterie Todt** is approximately half a mile down this road on the right-hand side. Parking is usually available in front of the museum. Access to abandoned *Türme* are through the wood directly ahead.

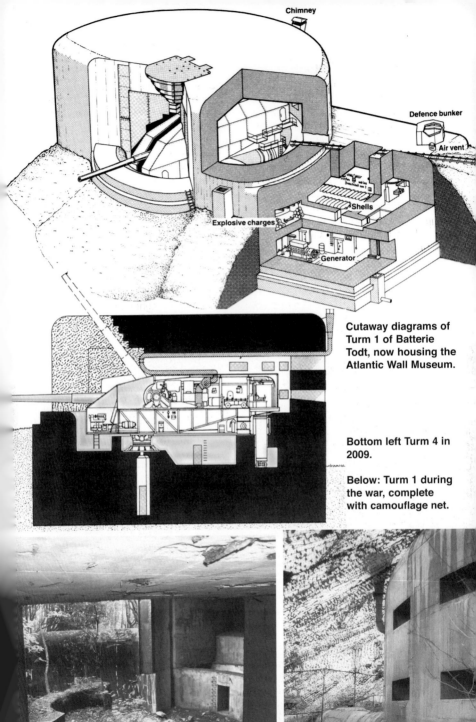

Chimney

Defence bunker

Air vent

Explosive charges

Shells

Generator

Cutaway diagrams of
Turm 1 of Batterie
Todt, now housing the
Atlantic Wall Museum.

Bottom left Turm 4 in
2009.

Below: Turm 1 during
the war, complete
with camouflage net.

7. La Trésorerie

Only Turm 2 of the Batterie Friedrich August is still accessible and the front of the bunker was completely destroyed in September 1944. But the rear entry is still intact and rooms on both levels can be reached, though largely gutted. On the ground floor, German graffiti is still visible on the walls.

Observation bunker at La Trésorerie.

The bunker is on private property and permision must be sought from the farm house situated near Turm 1 before entering the bunker.

Directions: From Calais, take the D940 onto the A16 heading for Boulogne. Leave the A16 at junction 33 signposted Wimille/Wimereux-Nord and take the D242 to La Tresorie.

6. La Coupole

La Coupole is a huge bunker built into a hillside on the site of an old quarry that was an intended launch site for V2 rockets in 1944.

Access to the museum is via a walkway through several large underground galleries and a lift. The site was bombed by the Allies and was never used as intended but the main control section has been converted into a state-of-the-art exhibition hall which has an interesting section on the occupation of the Pas de Calais, including relics, photographs and eye-witness accounts. There is also plenty of information about the Todt Organisation as well as the V1 and V2 *Vergeltungswaffen* Revenge weapons.

Directions: Found on the Rue Du Mont-a-Car at Hefault, just off the D210. The museum can be reached via either junction 3 or junction 4 off the A26 Calais to Paris route.

ACKNOWLEDGEMENTS

Without the help, direction and encouragement of the following, writing this book would not have been possible.

Firstly my wife Maria, who is responsible for much of the original photography in this volume, spent many hours translating documents and books for me and didn't complain about having to spend her summer holidays in museums or scrambling around ruined gun emplacements in northern France.

Thanks also to Simon for his original sketches, Henry Wilson, Roni Wilkinson and Rob Williams at Pen & Sword and the following individuals, institutions and points of reference for their previous research on Hitler's Atlantic Wall and associated sites as well as the military hardware of WWII.

In no particular order:

www.one35th.com" www.one35th.com

The Pill Box Study Group

The Unlikely Death of Patience Ransley by John Vaughan

Marilyn Stephenson-Knight at The Dover Memorial Project

Rolf-Dieter Muller

Objectif Douvres by Paul Gamelin (translated by Maria Williams)

The Tanks by Captain Sir Basil H. Liddell Hart

The Little-Known Story of Percy Hobart by Trevor J. Constable

The Victors: Eisenhower And His Boys: Men Of World War II
       by Stephen Ambrose

Remembering D-Day, Personal Histories of Everyday Heroes
       by Martin Bowman

www.worldwar2history.info

bundesarchiv

subterraneanhistory.co.uk

atlantikwall.tk

Canadian War Museum

The North Shore Regiment

Batterie Todt Museum, Audinghen

Smashing The Atlantic Wall by Patrick Delaforce (Pen & Sword)
The Atlantic Wall by Steven J Zaloga (Osprey Publishing)
The Story of the 79th Armoured Division Anon
The Encyclopedia of Weapons of World War II
        by Chris Bishop (Sterling Publishing)
La Coupole History and Remembrance Centre, St Omer
Royal Engineers Museum, Gillingham
Bovington Tank Museum
Normandy To The Baltic by Bernard Law Montgomery

Battle damage – bullet holes on a casemate at Wissant.

Chapter Nine

ATLANTIC WALL IN MAPS & PLANS

Hitler's Atlantic Wall garrison in 1944.

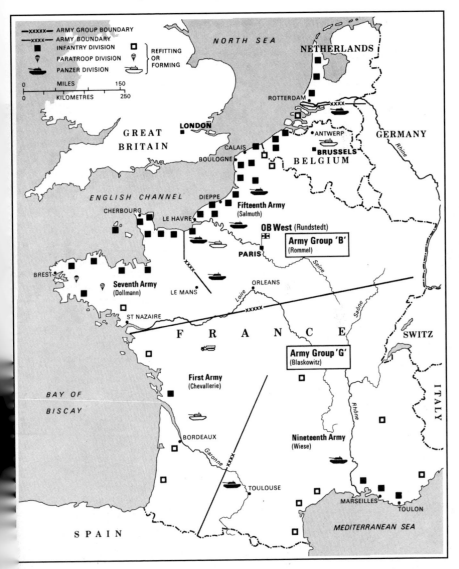

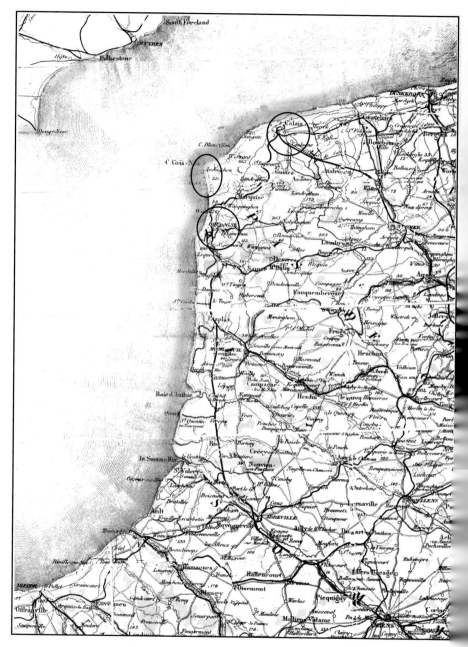

Area covered in the visitors' guide.

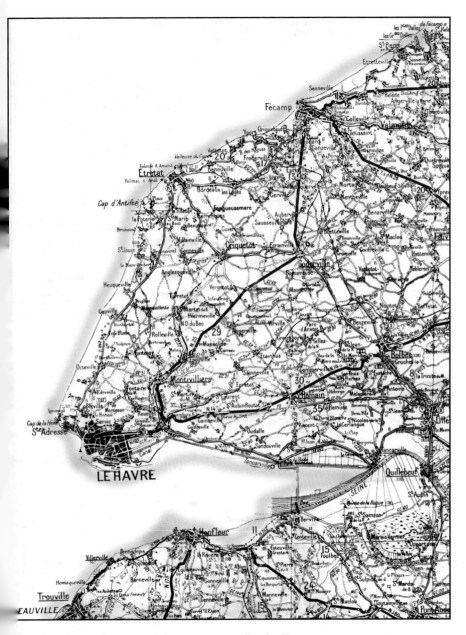

French war time map of the area surrounding Le Havre.

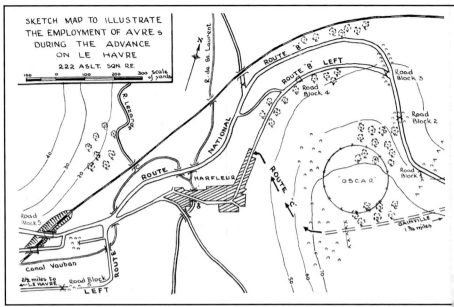

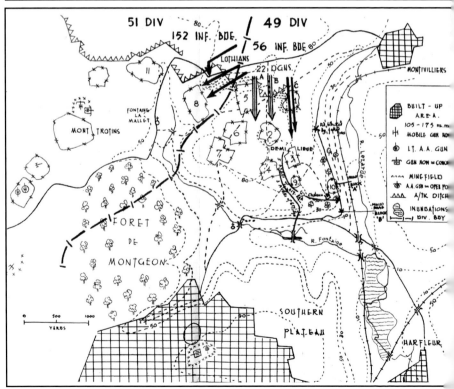

170

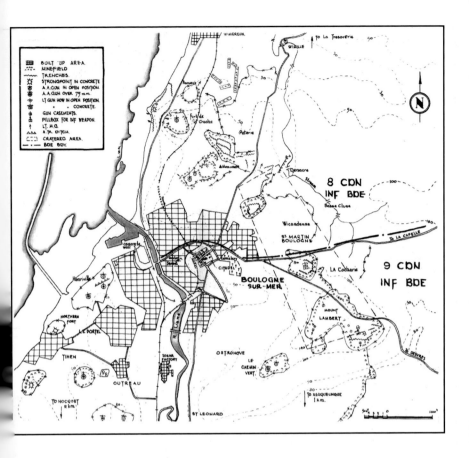

The assault on Boulogne.

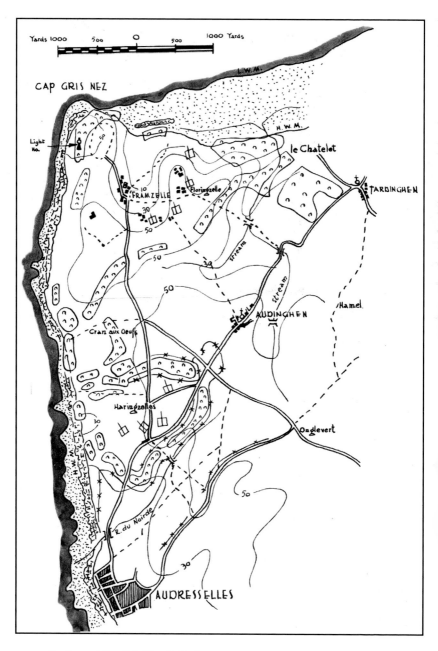

Capture of the Gris Nez Batteries.

172

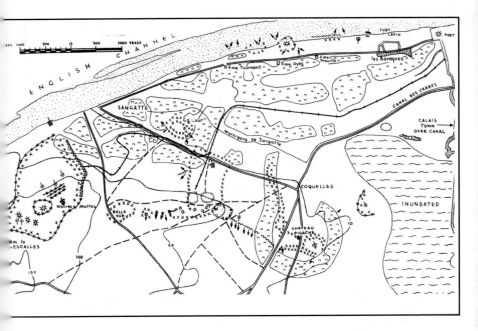

The assault on Calais.

INDEX

ARK	99
AVRE	93, 94, 97, 98, 114, 118, 121, 129, 131, 132, 137, 140
BARV	103
Batterie Friedrich August	142, 148
Batterie Lindemann	125, 132, 133, 137, 140
Batterie Kurfurst	125, 129, 131
Batterie Oldenburg	141
Batterie Todt	89, 90, 124, 131, 138, 140
Batterie Wissant	125
Belgian Gate	33
Bobbin	98
Boche Buster	25
Bodenstandige	36
Sir Alan Brooke	96, 102
Bullshorn	98
Canal Defence Light	105
Conger	137
Crab	97, 99, 111, 114, 129, 134, 137
Crocodile	99, 115, 118, 129, 137, 140
Czech Hedgehog	35
Dombunkers	17
Doppelgruppenstand	85
Xavier Dorsch	60
Double Onion	98
Duplex Drive	97, 99, 101, 102
Dwight Eisenhower	97, 104
Fan Bay	20, 23
Festung	62, 116, 146, 148, 156
Festungspionere	61, 76
Flying Dustbin	94, 97
Fort De La Creche	121
Fort des Dunes	146
Fort Nieulay	17
Fort Vert	88
Friedrich Frisius	147
Gastarbeitnehmer	47

Charles De Gaulle	146
Gold Beach	94
Hermann Göring	29
Gruppenstand	62
Hellfire Corner	18, 25
Hafenkommandant	65
Douglas Haig	91
Basil Liddell Hart	92, 106
General Ferdinand Heim	122
Heligoland	12, 13
Adolf Hitler	124
Percy Hobart	91, 92, 96, 97, 106
Home Guard	94
General Jodl	43
Juno Beach	72, 131, 123
Hans Kammler	60
Kampfgrubben	40
Kangaroos	111
Kriegsmarine	11, 12, 13, 30, 85, 86, 138, 148, 153
Krupp	13, 15
Lindemann Battery	26, 28, 89
Alois Liska	144
Luftwaffe	29, 30, 39, 45, 46, 148, 150
Maginot Line	9, 54, 76
Martin Mill	23
Erhard Milch	58
Minengranaten	36
Bernard Montgomery	97, 106
Oberkommando des Hees	38
Offene Bettung	63
Jack Olding	104
Omaha Beach	72, 150, 153
Operation Astonia	109, 115, 145
Operation Barbarossa	49
Operation Jubilee	64, 66
Operation Seelowe	9, 13, 31
Operation Undergo	124
Operation Wellhit	125, 135, 136
Organisation Todt	36, 45, 46, 48, 49, 56, 70, 72, 125
Ostbataillonen	38

Panzerkampwagen   73
Panzerstellung   71
Paris Gun   13, 15
Patience Ransle   26, 27
Pointe Du Hoc   86
RAF   101, 104, 109, 117, 121, 128, 140,
                            152, 156
Regelbau   70, 76
Reichsarbeitsdenst   46
Ringstand   61, 70
Erwin Rommel   36, 39, 40, 42, 44
Royal Artillery   20
Royal Engineers   92, 96
Royal Marine Siege Regiment 20
Royal Navy   65, 134
Fritz Sauckel   58
Kurt Schilling   140
Ludwig Schroeder   127, 129
William H Simpson   106
Sockellafetten   73
South Foreland   20
Albert Speer   57, 58, 64
Nicholas Straussler   101, 102, 103
Sword Beach   72
Teller Mine   34, 143
Fritz Todt   45, 46, 48, 50, 51, 52, 53, 55, 56,
                            57, 60, 146
Utah Beach   72, 152
Gerd von Runstedt   11, 42, 44, 150, 152-155, 158
Beyr von Schweppenburg   154
Georg von Sodenste   39, 40
Vestarkfeldmassig   63
Waffen-SS   148
Wanstone   20, 21, 22
Sir Archibald Wavell   92
Wehrmacht   9, 10, 13, 15, 18, 30, 45, 48, 72, 85,
                            88
Winston Churchill   19, 91, 92